Touring Albany
Fall

Copyright June 2019
ISBN
William (Bill) C. McElroy

Preface

This travel guide covers the state of New York from Albany west to Buffalo and Niagara Falls. The I-90 New York State Thruway is the prime east-west highway and the majority of the items that a tourist will want to see are with 25 miles of the exits.

The text is broken down into chapters that aid the reader in finding the particular item or place he or she wants to see or visit. All locations are listed alphabetically, and where possible have the street and town, plus zip and GPS address listed.

If you are traveling to an area, use the town or Zip code to search for additional items of interest in that area. Example if you search for *Zip Code 13027* you will find the *Beaver Lake Nature Center, Bud Light Amphitheater at Paper Mill Island, Erie Canal Lock 24, Mill Island Trail,* and the *Shacksboro Schoolhouse Museum.*

Please understand that the opening times and dates are up to the individual facilities, and thus may change at will. Many of the 750+ locations listed are seasonal and may not be open in the dead of winter. Also note that the suggested *'Plan on'* times are just that, suggested, and only provided so you can get an idea of your trip planning. You have to account for travel, travel delays, meals, crowds, and unforeseen delays and closures. *You have my disclaimer.*

Table of Contents

Chapter # 01 – Attractions

Most people know about New York City and many know about the Adirondacks, Niagara Falls, and the  Hudson Valley; each of which are major tourist destinations. What many do not know is that the area of New York State between the Hudson River at Albany and the Niagara River at Buffalo is rich in US history, in tourism attractions, in museums, and in vineyards.

There are several train rides, hiking trails, state parks, camping areas, lighthouses, forts, and RV parks throughout this part of the state; each is listed in this touring manual. Chapter # 01 covers the attractions that do not fall into many of the above categories.

Listed Alphabetically.

Albright-Knox Art Gallery

Closed on Mondays this 1862 art gallery features contemporary and masters artwork. If you wish to see works by *Francis Bacon, Frida Kahlo, Roy Lichtenstein, Georgia O'Keeffe, Pablo Picasso, Andy Warhol*, and others then this is the place. Plan on two or more hours.

1285 Elmwood Ave,
Buffalo, NY 14222

42.932459, -78.875624

Animal Adventure Park

You may not see elephants or Rhinos here, but they do have a large selection of both domestic and exotic animals, many of which you can pet and feed. Plan on two hours or more.

85 Martin Hill Road,
Harpursville, NY 13787
42.153908, -75.668073

Arlington Acres

This is a farm that was established in 1862 By D.W. & Elvira French, and has since 1904 been a place for *'romantic'* weddings. Yep, getting married in a barn on a farm does appeal to many, and this is one of the more *'favorable'* places to get *'hitched'*. Plan on one hour if visiting, several hours if getting married.

1155 Apulia Road,
Lafayette, NY 13084
42.827456, -76.078218

Beaver Lake Nature Center

The park has over a dozen hiking trails covering some nine (9) miles of wooded, meadow, swamp, and lake areas for your enjoyment. The best time to do this is probably in the late summer or early fall when the 'color' is at its prime. Plan on one to four or more hours.

8477 E Mud Lake Road,
Baldwinsville, NY 13027
43.180387, -76.399180

Binghamton Zoo

Ross Park Zoo

This is a typical display of wild animals, birds, and reptiles. Plan on three or more hours.

Binghamton Zoo at Ross Park
60 Morgan Road,
Binghamton, NY 13903
42.074999, -75.906975

Braddock Bay Bird Observatory

Opens at 6:30 am, and closes at 12:30 pm; this facility will show you how birds are *'banded'* so that each can be tracked over long periods of time. Plan on one hour.

10 Braddocks Ave,
Hilton, NY 14468
43.323379, -77.717429

Bud Light Amphitheater at Paper Mill Island

This amphitheater sits on Mill Island in the Seneca River. It is a place for concerts and other entertainments. Plan on 30-minutes to view, hours if attending a show.

Note that you are at Lock # 24 of the Erie Canal.

136 Spensieri Ave,
Baldwinsville, NY 13027
43.156377, -76.334120

Buffalo and Erie County Botanical Gardens

This 1900 Victorian glass structure houses hundreds of plants in 10 individual indoor greenhouses for your viewing enjoyment. The design is based on a similar building in England, the *Crystal Palace of England*. There are also in-season outdoor garden exhibits. Plan on three to four hours.

2655 South Park Ave,
Buffalo, NY 14218
42.828071, -78.825673

Buffalo Niagara Heritage Village

Closed on Monday and Tuesday this 35-acre museum village has costumed greeters and cultural festivals during times of the year. The complex has several buildings that have been moved to the site, including a schoolhouse, church, and blacksmith shop. Plan on four or more hours; many make it a full-days outing.

3755 Tonawanda Creek Road,
Amherst, NY 14228
43.084314, -78.729082

Campbell-Whittlesey House

Benjamin Campbell House

This is an 1836 Greek Revival home, designed by architect Minard Lafever. It was built for Mr. Campbell a Flour Miller.

Contact the *Landmark Society of Western New York* to see if it is for sale or sold, or still open as there were plans to close it.

Campbell - Whittlesey House
36 Troup Street,
Rochester, NY 14608
43.151228, -77.612292

Canalside

This is a Lake Erie Boardwalk area. Plan on an hour or more.

44 Prime Street,
Buffalo, NY 14202
42.876908, -78.879355

Capt. Samuel Maytan Fishing Access Site

Not really a tourist spot, but it is on the Mohawk River as it bypasses the *Erie Canal* in Herkimer. Be sure to have a fishing license if you do drop a line in the water.

413 S Washington Street,
Herkimer, NY 13350
43.018443, -74.978304

Caverns Creek Grist Mill

This 1816 mill uses the power of water to turn a 1,400-pound millstone as it grinds grains into flour. The mill did sell flour and other items, but it may not be in operation in 2019. It is still worth a drive by and a few pictures, open or not. Plan on 5 minutes.

259 Caverns Road,
Howes Cave, NY 12092
42.688542, -74.405457

C E Kenneth Mees Observatory

This space observatory is located 2260 ft above sea level in the Bristol Hills some 40 miles south of Rochester and is run by the *University of Rochester*. It is a teaching facility, and there are free tours Friday and Saturday nights during the months of June, July, and August.

6604 Gannett Hill Road,
Naples, NY 14512
42.700204, -77.408638

Clock Tower

This historic structure is in the center of an interesting shopping area in Corning New York, the home of *Corning Glass Works*. Plan on 10-minutes.

Center Way,
Corning, NY 14830
42.143727, -77.054319

CNY Living History Center

Closed on Mondays this facility has dozens of antique trucks, cars, tractors, and pieces of military equipment. Plan on two hours.

4386 US-11,
Cortland, NY 13045
42.619541, -76.183001

David A. Dimeo Memorial Labyrinth

Per the official website

> ""David was an engineer for the New York State Department of Transportation. He also spent many years leading and training countless Boy Scouts and Girl Scouts. He is remembered as being a loving husband, devoted father, loyal friend, teacher, engineer, Scout leader, mentor, NYSATE member and a lover of nature.
>
> "David succumbed to cancer in 1998. The labyrinth hopes to capture the multiple facets of his life; the geometry of engineering, the beauty of nature and the inspiring nature of his leadership.""

Plan on 15 to 30 minutes.

1525 Calkins Road,
Pittsford, NY 14534
43.068430, -77.574282

Devil's Bathtub Shelter

Mendon Ponds Park

This is a covered picnic area in the woods among the local lakes and many unnamed hiking trails. There are several of these shelter areas in *Mendon Ponds Park* including the *Alogonkian Shelter, Canfieldwoods Shelter, Southview Shelter, and Lookout Shelter*. Get there early, as it is a popular outdoor area for many that live in the area. Plan on one to several hours.

County Road 45,
Henrietta, NY 14467
43.023731, -77.573539

Discovery Center of the Southern Tier

This is a *'Children's Museum'* and play are near the *Binghamton Zoo*. Plan on one or more hours.

Discovery Center of the Southern Tier
60 Morgan Road,
Binghamton, NY 13903
42.073821, -75.903750

Dudley Observatory

This is an observatory for viewing the heavens and the stars above, and you are invited every day, and on Thursday nights. There is a planetarium and lots of displays. Plan on two to three hours.

15 Nott Terrace Heights,
Schenectady, NY 12308

42.811909, -73.933594

Elizabeth Cady Stanton House

Grassmere

Center of the Rebellion

1848 First Women's Rights Convention

Open Friday, Saturday, and Sunday this is the home of
Elizabeth Cady Stanton (1815-1902) who was
instrumental in the *Women's Movements* of the era. She
organized the *1848 First Women's Rights Convention* that
helped to eventually give women the right to vote as
well as other rights that women have gained and in
some instances still seek today. If you have the time,
look up the *Declaration of Sentiments*, which she co-
authored. Plan on one hour.

32 Washington Street,
Seneca Falls, NY 13148
42.912729, -76.788365

Endicott Visitors Center

Old Colonial Hall

Open Thursday, Friday, and Saturday from noon to
four this visitor center has a meeting room, gift shop,
and exhibits that feature the history of *Endicott Johnson
Shoe Company, IBM, Harpur College* and the *Endicott*
area. Plan on 30 minutes to an hour.

300 Lincoln Ave,
Endicott, NY 13760
42.098060, -76.051843

Erie Basin Marina Observation Deck

This is an observation deck high in a tower at the end of the pier that is part of the *Erie Basin Marina*. Plan on 30 to 45 minutes.

329 Erie Street,
Buffalo, NY 14202
42.884441, -78.889943

Flatman Sculpture

This is a 20-foot high metal sculpture that overlooks the river. Plan on 20 minutes to hike the park trail to it, and back.

Greenway Nature Trail,
Buffalo, NY 14203
42.859118, -78.875582

Flint House

Mohawk Valley Broomcorn Industry

Back in the 1840 era a broom was made from stalks of corn tied to a pole, and this area of New York was one of the major producers of *'Broomcorn'*, the type of corn that made the best brooms of the era. The *Flint House* is said to be the oldest house in Scotia and possibly the birthplace of the area's broomcorn industry. Plan on one hour.

421 S Reynolds Street,
Scotia, NY 12302
42.822860, -73.971876

Frank Lloyd Wright's Martin House Complex

Martin House

Closed on Tuesdays this is a 1905 home designed by *Frank Lloyd Wright* (1867-1959) for a wealthy businessman, *Darwin D. Martin; it* is one of many of Wright's excellent creations. Plan on one to two hours.

125 Jewett Pkwy,
Buffalo, NY 14214
42.936343, -78.847976

Frederick Douglass Resource

Per the guides.loc.gov website

"Frederick Douglass was a prominent African-American leader of the nineteenth century. He was an abolitionist, journalist, editor, political commentator, social critic, spiritual leader, and source of hope for the community of disenfranchised Americans."

This resource center provides the reader with many of Mr. Douglass's contributions to the cause of African Americans. Plan on one hour.

Frederick Douglass Resource
550 Clarissa Street # 101,
Rochester, NY 14608
43.145583, -77.617884

Gad Pierce Tavern Marker

During the War of 1812 this 1807 tavern built by Mr. Gad Pierce (June 12, 1768) was used to delay a British and Indian attack on the military. This happened in 1813 and was one of several tactics used by this tavern owner and military man to make the British think that there were far more US military than there really were. Plan on 10 minutes.

Niagara Falls, NY 14305
43.102001, -79.051662

Gell Center of the Finger Lakes

The Beagle

This is a 1929 estate of Dr. and Mrs. Kenneth Gell that has been turned into a *"Writer's"* retreat with excellent solitude and views of nature.

Gell Center of the Finger Lakes
6581 W Hollow Road,
Naples, NY 14512
42.698689, -77.420217

Gems Along the Mohawk

Mohawk Valley Visitors Center

This is a *Mohawk Valley Visitors Center* where you can obtain information about the area. Plan on 15 minutes.

800 Mohawk Street,
Herkimer, NY 13350
43.016949, -74.995983

Genesee Brew House

If you are a true New Yorker, then you know about Genesee Beer, it has been around for about a 100-years. This facility is a combination museum and pub where you can meet the Genesee Brewing Company people; learn about the making of fine beer, and much more including having a 'sample' or two. Plan on one or more hours.

Genesee Brew House
25 Cataract Street,
Rochester, NY 14605
43.163566, -77.614929

Greystone Castle

The original *Methodist Episcopal Church* burned to the ground in 1908 and was replaced by a White Marble church in 1909. This church stopped services in the 1960's and the building sat empty for about 30 years until it was converted to a commercial restaurant facility. Some of the original interior remains for your viewing pleasure. Plan on 30 minutes.

201 N Main Street,
Canastota, NY 13032
43.081230, -75.755076

Griffis Sculpture Park

This is a large field with some 250 pieces of 'Artwork' in the form of contemporary sculptures. The place is similar to *Storm King* in the Hudson Valley. *{See author's Hudson Valley and Vicinity Attractions – NYC's Playground}*

6902 Mill Valley Road,
East Otto, NY 14729
42.370128, -78.691555

Hang Gliding Launch

You will have to hike in and up, but the view is great and the glide can be fun. Plan on several hours.

Tully, NY 13159

42.792393, -76.043287

Hang Gliding Landing Area

Tully, NY 13159
42.795703, -76.054195

Harriet Tubman National Historical Park

Closed on Sunday and Monday. The *Underground Railroad* did NOT have any tracks; it was a series of very difficult pathways from the US south to the US north that escaping slaves used to find their freedom. *Ms Tubman* was instrumental in setting up the routes and helping bring slaves to freedom and to eventually get settled as free Americans.

She got along with the *'White wealthy'* and they helped her with her projects, something unheard of at that time, and pretty much today. Plan on one to two hours.

180 South Street,
Auburn, NY 13021
42.911374, -76.564496

Harriet Tubman Home

180 South Street,
Auburn, NY 13021
42.911551, -76.563736

Haunted House of Wax

This is not Ripley's believe it or not, and does not have wax figures of movie stars or political figures; it has skeletons, ghouls, and other creatures you do not want to meet in a dark alley. Plan on one hour.

222 Rainbow Blvd,
Niagara Falls, NY 14303
43.085823, -79.063186

Heritage Village of the Southern Finger Lakes

Closed on Sundays this village is a collection of buildings including a *1796 Benjamin Patterson Inn, 1878 Browntown Schoolhouse, 1870s Cooley Blacksmith Shop, 1850s Wixon Log Cabin, Painted Post RR station museum*, and several other buildings.

You will get to speak to and see actors in period garb doing the various work that was required of them during their time in history. Plan on four to six hours.

73 W Pulteney Street
Corning, NY 14830
42.151438, -77.063946

Herkimer Diamond Mines

From Official Website

"Herkimer Diamonds are beautiful double-terminated quartz crystals found in Herkimer, New York. Incredibly, these phenomenal gemstones are close to five hundred million years old. The crystals are magnificent works of nature, found in the rock, having a diamond-like geometrical shape. Thus, the name recognition of "Herkimer Diamonds""

Note that there is a KOA campsite across the street and they run the 'official' website.

Herkimer Diamond Mines
4601 NY-28,
Herkimer, NY 13350
43.128778, -74.976660

High Falls on the Genesee River at Rochester

This is a natural 96-foot high waterfall on the Genesee River in the city of Rochester. See the *Center at High Falls*, it provides a view of the falls and is a Historic district of Rochester.

New York
43.161392, -77.613587

High Falls Overlook

4 Commercial Street,
Rochester, NY 14614
43.161355, -77.614088

Historic Preservation

Historic Preservation is a National Park Service (NPS) operation that is attempting to preserve and protect our nation's history.

Peebles Island State Park Visitor Center

1 Delaware Ave, Cohoes, NY 12047
42.784010, -73.680712

10 Delaware Ave,
Cohoes, NY 12047
42.784471, -73.681172

Historic Trinity Church

This is an 1807 church and is one of several in the Middleville, New York and Fairfield, New York area. The others are the *St. Michael's Episcopal Church, Middleville Methodist Church, The Universalist Church, St. Mary's of the Assumption Roman Catholic Church*, and the *Methodist Church of Fairfield*, all of which were from the 1800s.

Plan on 15 to 30 minutes to see each.

Historic Trinity Church
808 NY-29,
Middleville, NY 13406
43.135936, -74.910846

Historic Valentown

Open Sundays from 1 to 4 pm this 1879 building is a part of the town's history and it is like stepping back in time as soon as you enter the doorway.

From Official Website.

> "In 1879, Levi and Alanson Valentine constructed the 4-story shopping plaza and community center (complete with underground parking!) on a busy crossstead homestead owned by their grandfather, Ichabod Town, hoping the property would be a stop on the Pittsburgh, Shawmut, and Northern Railroad.

> The landmark building is a rare example of 19th century architecture and has remained almost unaltered since its original construction. The inside remains much as it was when originally built: a general store, meeting room, bakery, harness shop, cobbler's shop, music school, display cases filled with early flags and military items, a Grange meeting room, railroad/trolley/telegraph office, ticket office and Grand Ballroom.

> Valentown is an intriguing Historical Museum containing literally thousands of artifacts, objects and heirlooms that represent the local 19th century history of the Victor and Rochester, New York area."

Plan on one to two hours.

267 High Street,
Victor, NY 14564
43.026112, -77.436398

Historical House

Castile Historical Society

This is an 1865 house built by Civil War veteran Henry L. Cumming. It is occupied by the *Castile Historical Society* and is a local historical museum.

17 Park Road W,
Castile, NY 14427
42.631362, -78.049320

Honeywell's Onondaga Lake Visitors Center

America's 'Most Polluted' Lake

 The Onondaga Lake in Syracuse, N.Y was polluted beyond help since 1898 due to industrial and municipal waste dumping. It took years for the cleanup, but today there are some 60 species of fish, and hundreds of birds.

{Picture is from Wikipedia and is of the 1900 Solvay Process Company, one of many companies that polluted the lake, it is public domain}

The site is a *Superfund site,* and Honeywell as one of the polluters is helping in the cleanup and prevention of even more {Mercury} pollution. The Visitor Center has descriptions of the problems and how each is being cleaned. Plan on 45 minutes.

280 Restoration Way,
Syracuse, NY 13209
43.073024, -76.204965

Howe Caverns

The author and his parents visited the caverns some 40 or 50 years ago and it became a 'memory' to not forget. You too can enjoy the hour tour and boat ride deep in the caverns exploring one of nature's most beautiful creations. Do bring a jacket, as it does get cool (~50 degrees F) during the tour. Plan on two to three hours total.

255 Discovery Drive,
Howes Cave, NY 12092
42.696250, -74.398639

Hyde Hall Covered Bridge

This single lane 53 foot 1825 wooden covered bridge is considered the oldest covered bridge in New York State. Plan on 15 minutes.

Glimmerglass State Park,
Cooperstown, NY 13326
42.790169, -74.863424

Indian Hunter Statue

John Quincy Adams Ward

This 1866 statue has been refurbished over the decades. John Quincy Adams Ward (1830–1910) *"the dean of American sculptors"* created the statue that shows a young Native American with bow holding back his dog as he hunts for his family's food. Plan on 5 minutes.

Delaware Park,
Buffalo, NY 14214
42.932441, -78.855173

International Boxing Hall of Fame

If you are a 'Boxing' fan, then you will certainly enjoy your hour or more visit to this facility. There are full-size figures of famous boxers, lots of gloves, shirts, plaques, and other history of the sport.

360 N Peterboro Street,
Canastota, NY 13032
43.089591, -75.750095

It's a Wonderful Life Bridge

George Bailey Bridge

It's a Wonderful Life

Although never proven, the town of Seneca Falls closely resembled the town of Bedford Falls in Frank Capra's holiday classic movie *"It's A Wonderful Life."* Due to this, the assumption is that this bridge is the bridge that George Bailey stood on and contemplated suicide.

Next to the bridge is the *Ludovico Sculpture Trail* and a few blocks north is the *Women's Rights National Historical Park*.

Plan on 15 minutes at the bridge location.

Seneca Falls, NY 13148
42.909421, -76.800797

Johnson Hall State Historic Site

Superintendent of Indian Affairs

Open late on Sunday, closed on Monday and Tuesday. This 1763 Georgian-style estate was the property of *Sir William Johnson (1715 - 1774) and Molly Brant.* Mr. Johnson was an Irish immigrant and his marriage to Ms. Brant a Mohawk Indian produced eight children. While living in the estate his interaction with the natives earned him the title of *Superintendent of Indian Affairs,* he got along with the Iroquois (Six Nations) and helped England to win the war with France that gave control of colonial North America to England.

After his death in 1774 Mrs. Johnson moved to Canada, and the estate was left to the oldest child, and eventually sold at auction. In 1906 New York State acquired it and today it is a tourist site with picnic grounds, gift shop, and museum. Plan on two hours.

139 Hall Ave,
Johnstown, NY 12095
43.016354, -74.383477

Kateri Tekakwitha Marker

Lily of the Mohawks

This roadside marker is a pyramid of cemented stones that honors *Catherine Tekakwitha* (1656 – April 17, 1680). She was born in the Mohawk village of Ossernenon; she lost her parents to smallpox, and she herself was disfigured. She has a history of doing miracles and was eventually canonized by Pope Benedict XVI at Saint Peter's Basilica on 21 October 2012. She is considered a 'Saint'; and she obtained the nickname the *Lily of the Mohawks*.

Amsterdam, NY 12010
42.927830, -74.303722

LaSalle Waterfront Park

Local park on the shore of the Niagara River. Good rest area just off of I-190 as you enter the US from Canada. There are a picnic area, restrooms (part of year), and good views of the *North Grand Island Bridge* and the *Niagara River*. Plan on 15 minutes to an hour.

6611 Buffalo Ave,
Niagara Falls, NY 14304
43.074282, -78.988016

Lincoln Baths

Farmer's Market

Today there is a Farmer's Market at this site, but before 1909 there were wells producing Carbon Dioxide gas that was used for soda production. In 1915 the spa building was constructed to take advantage of the springs that were there after the gas production was hauled. In 1927 the wooden building burnt to the ground and in 1929 was replaced with the new stone, steel, terracotta, and concrete building said at the time to be the largest *'spa'* building in the world.

The building was the first building in what is now the *Saratoga SPA State Park*. Plan on two hours.

65 S Broadway,
Saratoga Springs, NY 12866
43.064689, -73.790202

Little House

This is an 1819 Federal style architecture home used for a professional office, a bakery, a nursery school, and a travel agency. Plan on 15 minutes.

18 Monroe Ave,
Pittsford, NY 14534
43.091391, -77.516819

Little Joe Tower

Corning Glass Company

Remember glass thermometers? Well to 'draw' the glass into long tubes the *Corning Glass Company* constructed a 185-foot tall tower where the hot-plasticized glass could be drawn with a hair-thickness inner cavity for the liquid mercury used. You cannot enter the tower, but it stands as a monument to the ingenuity of engineers and designer of the 1912 era thermometer tubing production facility.

Chestnut Street,
Corning, NY 14830
42.145268, -77.057721

Little Lady Liberty

Lady Liberty greets you as you come over the Rainbow Bridge from Canada. Plan on 5 minutes.

413 Main Street,
Niagara Falls, NY 14301
43.088559, -79.063425

Mabee Farm Historic Site

Closed on Sunday and Monday this rural farm is open for inspection and for special events.

Per Wikipedia

The original structures on the farm are the stone house, a frame pre-Erie Canal inn, in which Revolutionary War General Philip Schuyler stayed in 1792 while surveying for the Western Inland Navigation and Lock Company, and the half brick house. The farm's original barns, however, were consumed by fire in the 1870s and 1970s. There is also a family cemetery, which has 21 headstones dating from 1771, including a recent (2011) marker honoring the slaves owned by the Mabee family

The Mabee Farm Historic Site is open year-round to visitors for guided tours through the historic structures, and/or for self-guided visits through the exhibits on display in the Franchere Center. Special events take place from May through October. In 2016, those events include the Migration Celebration, Celtic Heritage Day, Revolutionary War Living History Weekend, CanalFest, Arts & Crafts Festival, and the Fall Foliage Festival.

Plan on two or more hours.

1100 Main Street,
Rotterdam Junction, NY 12150
42.864722, -74.031771

Max Farash Center for Observational Astronomy

Be sure to consult their website calendar for 'open house' days and events. They have several telescopes, and you can join them on certain days (Nights) for observing the galaxy and the stars. Plan on two to four hours.

Meteorites

Langheinrich Fossil Preserve Inc

Small museum and store for showing and selling meteorites.

Meteorites
290 Brewer Road,
Ilion, NY 13357
42.960218, -75.065769

Millard Fillmore Birthplace Cabin (Replica)

Fillmore Glen State Park

President Millard Fillmore (1800 - 1874) was born in this log cabin (Recreated) and the cabin is partly furnished with the furniture and items of the era. Plan on 10 to 15 minutes at the cabin, and an hour or more walking the grounds. There is camping, hunting; swimming, picnicking, and hiking trail areas for you enjoyment.

Fillmore Glen State Park

Moravia, NY 13118
42.698227, -76.416543

Mills Mansion

Open on Saturday and Sunday this is the home of the first citizen of Mt. Morris, a Major General William Augustus Mills (1777-1844). General Mills built the 1836 (Disputed 1838) Federal style house and it is now being used as the Mount Morris Historical Society headquarters. General Mills lead troops in the war of 1812. Plan on one to two hours. Note: The website on Google for this location takes you to the NYS website and the wrong Mills estate (May 31, 2019).

14 Main Street
Mt Morris, NY 14510
42.726833, -77.875133

Mohawk Valley Welcome Center - Westbound

This is a stop on the Interstate I-90 where you can relax for a while and get some information about the Mohawk Valley and its attractions. Plan on 15 minutes.

I-90 Westbound Milepost 187,
Fultonville, NY 12072
42.916231, -74.446649

Montezuma National Wildlife Refuge

This wildlife refuge is large and has three lakes, a waterway, several hiking trails, a visitor center and some observation areas where you may see bald eagles, herons, egrets, and other birds. It is a great place for birdwatchers, hikers, and nature lovers to visit. If you do not want to hike it; then you can listen to your car radio as it describes the attractions on your self-driving tour. Plan on one to several hours.

3395 Hwy 20,
Seneca Falls, NY 13148
42.962656, -76.740937

Centennial Viewing Platform – Bird Watching

Seneca Trail,
Seneca Falls, NY 13148
42.969736, -76.739993

Observation Tower

Seneca Trail,
Seneca Falls, NY 13148
42.969346, -76.740255

Visitor Center And Lodge Nature Store

3396 Hwy 20,
Seneca Falls, NY 13148
42.966972, -76.740817

Munson-Williams-Proctor Arts Institute

Open late on Sunday, closed on Mondays. Rotating selections of art and other artistic entertainment provide an enchanting visit to this one of a kind art museum/complex.

From official website

> "The Institute is named for three generations of one Utica, NY family. Alfred Munson (1793-1854), who moved from Connecticut in 1823, accumulated the initial family fortune from industrial interests in the Northeast, including the manufacturing of burrstones and textiles, coalmines, canal development, and railroad and steamboat transportation. He and his wife, Elizabeth, had two children, Helen (1824-94) and Samuel (1826-81)."

Plan on two or more hours.

310 Genesee Street,
Utica, NY 13502
43.097570, -75.240169

National Distance Running Hall

Boilermaker Road Race Corporate Office

This is foot race and the location has the history of prior winners.

Boilermaker Road Race Corporate Office

805 Court Street,
Utica, NY 13502
43.102709, -75.244525

National Women's Hall of Fame

Helen M. Barben

1844 Seneca Knitting Mill

This is a history of women in their quest for recognition and rights and the *Helen M. Barben* building is near the corner where the placard states:

> *"First Convention for Woman's Rights was held on this corner 1848".*

The displays include awards, descriptive history, clothing, some full size figures, and more. There are plans in 2019 to move to the *1844 Seneca Knitting Mill*, which is located on 1 Canal Street in Seneca Falls

76 Fall Street,
Seneca Falls, NY 13148
42.910647, -76.797459

New York City Architectural Model

Open daily from 9 to 9 this is a room size miniature of the city and suburbs of New York City. The detail is astonishing, and it is a must see if you are in the Schenectady area. Plan on 30 minutes.

Rotterdam, NY 12306

42.809141, -73.988009

New York State Fairgrounds

For 2019 the fair dates are Aug. 21 - Sep. 2, 2019

581 State Fair Blvd,
Syracuse, NY 13209
43.073230, -76.224744

Observation Tower – Seneca Falls

This is in the *Montezuma National Wildlife Refuge* and allows for views of the lake and the birds that live in the area. Plan on one or more hours.

Seneca Trail,
Seneca Falls, NY 13148
42.969349, -76.740257

Olcott Beach Carousel Park

Opens at noon, but is closed on Mondays and Tuesdays. This Ontario Lake, Lakeside Park has shops, the carousel, and a lighthouse. Plan on spending several hours.

5979 E Main Street,
Olcott, NY 14126
43.338526, -78.713358

Old Jello Factory

The building is unoccupied and is closed to the public, but it is a bit of history of the place where Jello was manufactured. From a roadside marker sign comes the following:

In 1897, Pearle Bixby Wait of LeRoy, introduced a gelatin dessert that his wife, May, named JELL-O. The first four flavors were strawberry, raspberry, orange and lemon. In 1899, he began production of JELL-O in a factory building located near this site. On September 9, 1899 he sold the rights to JELL-O to the Genesee Pure Food Company of LeRoy for $450.

Old Jello Factory
Le Roy, NY 14482
42.984727, -77.984123

Oneida County History Center

Closed Saturday and Sunday this county history center has both permanent and temporary displays that date from the recent past back decades. Plan on one to two hours.

1608 Genesee Street,
Utica, NY 13502
43.091464, -75.252365

Orin Lehman Visitor Center

This visitor center may have tickets to some of the rides and events, a restroom, and a small museum with some history of the area and the falls. Plan on 15 minutes to one-half hour.

Niagara Falls Visitor Center,
Niagara Falls, NY 14303
43.086302, -79.066425

Paige's Butterfly Garden

Hope for the Bereaved

This is a quiet spot along *Onondaga Lake* where people come to remember their departed loved ones. While in the area visit the *Salt Museum* and the *Skä•noñh Great Law of Peace Center*.

Plan on 15 minutes.

6571-6733 Onondaga Lake Pkwy,
Liverpool, NY 13088
43.095994, -76.200880

Palatine German Frajlkkme House

This is a 1760 Post and Beam farmhouse; it is not open to the public, but has been designated a landmark. Plan on 2 minutes.

4217 NY-5,
Frankfort, NY 13340
43.029013, -75.043591

Play Space ABC Cayuga

Open late on Sundays, closed on Monday and Tuesday this facility has play items for toddlers and the very young. Plan on an hour or more.

63 Genesee Street,
Auburn, NY 13021
42.932088, -76.565914

Reinstein Center

Julia Boyer Reinstein Center

This is a small museum near the local art centers and the *Buffalo History Museum*.

From the Official website:

> "The building was named after *Julia Boyer Reinstein*. Dedicated to both history and libraries, Julia Boyer Reinstein served as the Cheektowaga town historian for many years and was active in the creation of numerous town historical societies across WNY."

Plan on 20 to 30 minutes.

4 Elmwood Ave,
Buffalo, NY 14201
42.935208, -78.877486

Riverlink Park

This is a local park on the banks of the Mohawk River; it has a boat landing area, and two overhead walkways, one over the railroad tracks and the other over the river. It is near the *Kirk Douglas Park* and his *childhood home*. There is ample parking on both sides of the river, but you will have to walk to the park area.

2 Front Street,
Amsterdam, NY 12010
42.934180, -74.191565

Kirk Douglas' Childhood House

46 Eagle Street,
Amsterdam, NY 12010
42.929832, -74.181674

Mohawk Valley Gateway Overlook
Pedestrian Bridge

1 Bridge Street,
Amsterdam, NY 12010
42.935322, -74.195427

West End WWI Memorial

Amsterdam, NY 12010
42.934103, -74.197067

Rome Sports Hall of Fame

This sports hall of fame tells the stories of the athletes of Rome, New York, and especially the feats and accomplishments of the female athletes. Plan on one hour.

5790 Rome-New London Road,
Rome, NY 13440
43.226198, -75.503261

Rosamond Gifford Zoo

This zoo will take four or more hours to see, so wear good walking shoes, sunscreen, and enjoy the day.

1 Conservation Place,
Syracuse, NY 13204

43.043353, -76.181079

Round Lake National Natural Landmark

Green Lake State Park

This is one of the two ancient lakes at *Green Lake State Park*; there is a beach at Green Lake, and there are hiking trails. Round lake (185 feet deep) is a rare *Meromictic* lake that is surrounded by a forest that dates back to at least 1855 (probably much older).

A Meromictic lake is one in which it is deep enough (55 feet) so that the surface water does not mix with the bottom oxygen deprived waters.

Plan on one or more hours.

Manlius, NY 13066
43.049000, -75.973010

Green Lake Beach

Fayetteville, NY 13066
43.058030, -75.964217

Salmon River Fish Hatchery

Many people think of Salmon as a Pacific fish that is off the coast of Oregon and in the Columbia River, and yes that is one of many places where Salmon can be caught or raised, but Lake Ontario is also a place for catching Salmon. The Salmon River flows into the lake and this Hatchery is on the river some 12.5 miles inland. You can tour the hatchery and see how the fish are raised and eventually released into the river. Plan on one hour.

2133 County Rte 22,
Altmar, NY 13302
43.510126, -75.992106

Saratoga Harness Hall of Fame

If you have not been to a Harness Race you are in for a treat as the horses pull the two-wheel *'Roman Style'* wagons around the track. This small museum has the *'Silk'*, the horseshoes, and the history of some of the notable winning horses and riders. Plan on an hour.

352 Jefferson Street,
Saratoga Springs, NY 12866
43.061017, -73.778248

Schoellkopf Power Station

Now part of the Niagara Falls State Park this 1905 power station is open to the public. You can travel to the base of the station by elevator and admire the construction of the towers that contained the water driven generators.

This 1905 power station has more than three sections, Station 3B was built in the 1918 to 1920 era and Station 3C was built in the 1921 to 1924 era. The six Niagara River generators were fed by canal diverted river water and produced 322,500 horsepower up to June 7, 1956 when a rockslide put each out of operation. Plan on two hours.

Niagara Falls, NY 14303
43.092582, -79.062620

Schuyler Mansion State Historic Site

Open Wednesday - Sunday, 11:00 a.m. to 5:00 P.M. This 1765 Georgian Style Schuyler Mansion was the home of *Major General Philip Schuyler* and *Catharine van Rensselaer Schuyler*. Their daughter *Eliza Schuyler* married *Alexander Hamilton* at the mansion in 1780. Plan on two hours.

32 Catherine Street,
Albany, NY 12202
42.641478, -73.759381

Seabreeze Amusement Park

This 1872 amusement park is the 4th-oldest in the nation and has been upgraded to provide the latest in thrills and rides, so be ready to spend several hours. Note that their website should be consulted as there are many rules and regulations that apply.

4600 Culver Road,
Rochester, NY 14622

43.232054, -77.542408

Secret Caverns

This 1928 discovery is not far from *Howes Caverns* and offers a slightly rougher and more interesting experience as it is damp, i.e. somewhat slippery, and there are some 100 steps to maneuver on your tour to the *underground waterfall*. There are guides and a gift shop. Plan on two or more hours.

671 Caverns Road,
Howes Cave, NY 12092
42.709602, -74.391949

Skä·nonh-Great Law of Peace Center

Closed on Monday and Tuesday this facility has displays and history of the Native American Indians of central New York. Plan on two hours, and be sure to go out back to see the village.

Liverpool, NY 13088
43.093542, -76.196895klj

Spiritualist Obelisk

Small park with obelisk.

49 Troup Street,
Rochester, NY 14608
43.151258, -77.613463

Strasenburgh Planetarium

Closed on Mondays.
From official website

"Our public programs include:

Immersive Featured Presentations and Star Shows that feature "Carl," our legendary star projector, and our new Digistar 6 full dome visualization system.

Themed Saturday Night Laser Shows that combine classic rock music with groovy and dazzling laser light effects (Will return by popular demand on Saturday, Feb. 2, 2019!)

Free public telescope viewing on the Planetarium roof! Telescope viewing is offered on Saturday evenings (weather permitting) thanks to volunteers from the Astronomy Section of the Rochester Academy of Science."

663 East Ave,
Rochester, NY 14607
43.152116, -77.586760

Ten Broeck Mansion

Closed on Monday, Tuesday, and Wednesday, check for opening times. This 1797 mansion has beautiful gardens, fine furnishings, and lots of history. Take the tour. Plan on one to two hours.

9 Ten Broeck Place,
Albany, NY 12210
42.658734, -73.751162

The Buffalo Zoo

It's a zoo, it has animals for you to see. Plan on three to four or more hours.

300 Parkside Ave,
Buffalo, NY 14214
42.937154, -78.851610

The Site of the First Gas Well Marker

This marker is on a rock between two stone posts across the street from the local firehouse.

Fredonia, NY 14063
42.438212, -79.333744

Tinker Nature Park/Hansen Nature Center

Closed on Sunday and Monday this 68-acre park features some nature trails and the *Tinker Homestead & Farm Museum*. Plan on one or more hours.

Tinker Nature Park/Hansen Nature Center
1525 Calkins Road,
Pittsford, NY 14534
43.067611, -77.574843

Tinker Homestead & Farm Museum

1585 Calkins Road,

Pittsford, NY 14534
43.068608, -77.575407

Tipperary Hill Traffic Light

Stone Throwers Park

This upside down traffic light is in what is known as
'Little Ireland' in Syracuse New York. The original light
was *'Red'* over *'Green'* like all others in the US, but the
Irish in the neighborhood decided that the *'Green'*
should be *'Over the Red'*, and thus. ..

"Stone Throwers" park was built in 1997 and has statues
of those that 'threw' stones at the 1920's light thus
continuously breaking the *'Red'* lens until the *'Green'*
was installed over the *'Red'*. Plan on 20 minutes with
trying to find a place to park.

106-14 Burnet Park Drive,
Syracuse, NY 13204
43.046549, -76.185573

Tonawanda Castle

Closed on Sunday

Per official website

"The history of the Tonawanda Castle is both unique and powerful. Constructed as an armory for the 25th Separate Company of the National Guard, the massive 38,000 square-foot armory was built in the impressively short span of half a year, between the winter of 1896 and summer of 1897. With a foundation of Warsaw blue granite and walls of deep red mason brick, this historic building has presided over Delaware Street in the city of Tonawanda for more than 100 years.

Now renovated into a captivating event space, Tonawanda Castle still has the power to take its guests back in time for a wondrous night."

Plan on 30 minutes to view the architecture, and hours if attending an event.

69 Delaware Street,
Tonawanda, NY 14150
43.017257, -78.873561

Tribes Hill Heritage Center

This Native American enterprise is part of the history of New York State and is a must visit for those that wish to learn more.

From the official website:

"We have found the perfect location

Hello friends of THHC, just wanted to give you all an update on our progress thus far. We are pleased to announce that we have selected 55 acres in the Town of Florida to be the future home of The Tribes Hill Heritage Center. Currently we are negotiating the zoning aspects of the purchase. We will keep you apprised of further news. Please use our P.O. Box address (Tribes Hill Heritage Center P.O. Box 377, Tribes Hill, NY 12177) for correspondence or private message and someone will be in touch with you as soon as possible.

Thank you all for your continued support.

Tribes Hill Heritage Center"

Plan on one hour.

Rotterdam, NY 12306
42.808372, -73.988852

Underground Railroad History Project of the Capital Region, Inc.

Closed on Sundays. This 2003 formed organization is attempting to salvage buildings, artifacts, and the history of the UGR (Underground Railroad) in the Albany, New York area. Plan on one hour.

194 Livingston Ave,
Albany, NY 12210

42.661151, -73.754374

VIA Aquarium

This is a small, by other aquarium standards, child friendly aquarium that is doing its best to expand and become the 'place' to take your children for a few hours of entertainment, excitement, and education of nature and its wonders. Plan on one to two hours.

93 W Campbell Road,
Schenectady, NY 12306
42.808771, -73.986160

Vintage Drive In-Theater

Remember the days of necking while pretending to watch the movie in a 'Drive-in' theater, well those days are still with us as this is one of the few drive-in theaters still operating in the nation. There are four (4) screens, and you get to see two movies for the entry price. There is also miniature golf and a snack bar. Plan on two to four hours.

1520 W Henrietta Road,
Avon, NY 14414
42.915045, -77.707513

Watkins Glen International Speedway

This famous automotive racetrack is open for your enjoyment to watch drivers test their vehicles as the circle the track; then for a fee you get to take three laps behind a pace car in your vehicle. Plan on one to three hours.

2790 County Route 16,
Watkins Glen, NY 14891
42.338300, -76.926355

Weslyan Methodist Chapel

Women's Rights National Historical Park

Per the NPS website:

> "The Wesleyan Chapel was built in 1843.
> On July 19 and 20, 1848, the **First
> Women's Rights Convention** was held
> here. Even though **Elizabeth Cady
> Stanton** was the only one of the five
> organizers to live in Seneca Falls, the
> Wesleyan Chapel was well known to them
> all. The church was a local haven for
> antislavery activity, political rallies, and
> free speech events.
>
> The original red brick Wesleyan Methodist
> Church was sold by the congregation in
> 1871 and extensively altered by subsequent
> owners. When the site was purchased by
> the National Park Service in 1985, very
> little original fabric remained. The site
> today offers a unique display of the
> highlighted historic fabric of the original
> building."

Plan on one hour.

Seneca Falls, NY 13148
42.910782, -76.799687

Women's Rights National Historical Park

This park features the Weslyan Methodist Chapel where in July 19-20,1848 the first Women's Rights Convention was held. The participants *Thomas and Mary M'Clintock, Elizabeth C. Stanton, Lucretia Mott, Ansel Bascom, S.E. Woodworth, Amy Post, Catharine Stebbins, Martha C. Wright*, and *James Mott* authored and adopted the *"Declaration of Sentiments"*. A room size statue exists that represents this group. Plan on an hour or more.

136 Fall Street,
Seneca Falls, NY 13148
42.910758, -76.800201

Woods Valley Ski Area

Closed on Mondays and Tuesdays. The facility has a Tap Bar and several lifts and downhill trails. Plan on several hours of skiing.

9100 NY-46,
Westernville, NY 13486
43.302680, -75.384761

Chapter # 02 – Beaches

Lake Erie and Lake Ontario border the western area of New York State and there are also many very good lakes within the state that may be suitable for swimming, boating, or fishing. The following are some of the many beaches that you may seek out to enjoy a day of relaxation.

Barcelona Harbor Beach – Lake Erie

8298 1st Street,
Westfield, NY 14787
42.340920, -79.599423

Green Lake Beach

Fayetteville, NY 13066
43.058023, -75.964225

Eagle Bay beach

Silver Creek, NY 14136
42.535789, -79.223500

Evangola Beach

Erie County

New York
42.608483, -79.112239

Mendon Ponds Beach Parking Lot

Henrietta, NY 14467
43.028395, -77.558212

Manitou Beach Preserve

64 Manitou Beach Road,
Hilton, NY 14468
43.321706, -77.715268

Perry Public Beach

42 Walker Road,
Perry, NY 14530
42.706272, -78.022153

Woodlawn Beach

Erie County
New York 14219
42.789312, -78.853142

Chapter # 03 – Campgrounds

Campgrounds are scattered across the state of New York, and many will accommodate RV's, horses, dogs, etc. Most are 'tent' or 'cabin' camping, and have limited resources for RV's, thus *see the Chapter on RV Parks for RV camping.*

 Some of the State and local parks may have tent, RV, or both camping. *See Chapter on State & Federal Parks.* Note that not all parks or campgrounds have the facilities for electrical, water, or sewer hookups that most RV owners require.

Here are some of the many New York State campgrounds you might consider staying at.

{Picture is from Wikipedia, author Ebedgert. It is from a campsite on Green Lake, it is public domain}

Backbone Horse Camp

Picnic Area Road,
Burdett, NY 14818
42.485260, -76.806883

Beulah Park Campground

1035 County Rte 48,
Richland, NY 13144
43.564599, -76.052128

Blueberry Patch Campground

Picnic Area Road,
Burdett, NY 14818

42.484264, -76.808759

Camp Brockway Reservations

7673 Pratts Falls Road,
Manlius, NY 13104
42.933442, -75.988208

Camp Stella Maris

4395 E Lake Road,
Livonia, NY 14487
42.804882, -77.701697

Cider House Campground

3570 Canal Road,
Bouckville, NY 13310
42.892758, -75.548108

Conesus Lake Campground

5609 E Lake Road,
Conesus, NY 14435
42.748782, -77.712298

ConTENTment Camping

9691 Lower Lake Road,
Barker, NY 14012
43.365526, -78.482681

Cooperstown Beaver Valley Cabins & Campsites

Cooperstown Beaver Valley Cabins & Campsites
138 Towers Road,
Milford, NY 13807
42.653000, -74.999122

Cooperstown Deer Run Campground

7489 NY-80,
Cooperstown, NY 13326
42.820997, -74.891940

Cooperstown KOA Journey

Cooperstown KOA Journey
565 Ostrander Road,
Richfield Springs, NY 13439
42.852554, -74.890927

Cooperstown Shadow Brook Campground

Cooperstown Shadow Brook Campground
2149 Co Road 31,
Cooperstown, NY 13326
42.816623, -74.825630

Edgewater Seasonal Campground

2253 Lakeshore Drive,
Blossvale, NY 13308
43.223660, -75.735833

Gardner Hill Campground

1451 Norway Road,
Lowman, NY 14861
42.076010, -76.701385

Herkimer Diamond KOA Resort

Herkimer Diamond KOA Resort
4626 State Route 28
North, Herkimer, NY 13350
43.127218, -74.975962

Hide-a-Way Campsites

107 Janice Lane
Central Bridge, NY 12035
42.729661, -74.363990

Hidden Point Campground

1010 Waterview Drive,
Blossvale, NY 13308
43.210540, -75.714288

Hidden Valley 4-H Camp

Hidden Valley Camp Road,
Watkins Glen, NY 14891
42.362834, -76.920907

Lone Pine Campgrounds

600 16th Ave,
Sylvan Beach, NY 13157

43.203686, -75.724098

Mayfair Campground

3250 Old State Rte 49,
Blossvale, NY 13308
43.235893, -75.671316

Montour Falls Marina Campground

97 Marina Drive,
Montour Falls, NY 14865
42.353875, -76.852628

Nine Mile Island Camping Area

25-355 Orbit Drive,
Buffalo, NY 14228
43.070879, -78.739647

Paradise Cove Campground

7201 Cove Road,
Durhamville, NY 13054
43.210148, -75.710924

Pulaski Historical Society

3428 Maple Ave,
Pulaski, NY 13142
43.568263, -76.125021

Richland Holiness Camp

1035 County Rte 48,

Richland, NY 13144
43.564801, -76.053734

River Forest Park Campground

9439 Riverforest Road,
Weedsport, NY 13166
43.074589, -76.564810

Southern Adirondack Pines Campground
& Cabins

153 Pine Lake Road,
Caroga Lake, NY 12032
43.192436, -74.521616

Southern Shores Campgrounds

5707 E Lake Road,
Conesus, NY 14435
42.743986, -77.709344

Spruce Row Campsite

2271 Kraft Road,
Ithaca, NY 14850
42.516935, -76.588019

TA-GA-SOKE Campgrounds

7820 Higginsville Road,
Blossvale, NY 13308
43.224618, -75.698180

The Landing Campground

2796 Kellogg Road,
Blossvale, NY 13308
43.221597, -75.702930

Upper Delaware Campgrounds

36 Upper Delaware Camp Road,
Callicoon, NY 12723
41.759814, -75.055160

Watkins Glen / Corning KOA Resort

1710 NY-414,
Watkins Glen, NY 14891
42.315423, -76.907748

Western New York Camping

6994 Plato Road #2,
East Otto, NY 14729
42.350257, -78.700073

White Birch Campground

7945 Lake Road,
Sodus Point, NY 14555
43.269082, -77.007849

Chapter # 04 – Casinos

New York State has several casinos where you can bet on horses, use slot machines, and play card games.

{Picture is from Wikipedia, author Rodw, it is public domain}

Some of these are on Native American lands, and some have restaurants, conference rooms, and hotel suites. Here are a few you may consider.

Batavia Downs Gaming

8315 Park Road,
Batavia, NY 14020
43.009425, -78.205147

del Lago Resort & Casino

1133 NY-414,
Waterloo, NY 13165
42.970152, -76.845438

Finger Lakes Gaming & Racetrack

5857 NY-96,
Farmington, NY 14425
42.971719, -77.343664

Point Place Casino

450 NY-31,
Bridgeport, NY 13030
43.154200, -75.967633

Rivers Casino & Resort Schenectady

1 Rush Street,
Schenectady, NY 12305
42.823394, -73.935935

Saratoga Casino Hotel

342 Jefferson Street,
Saratoga Springs, NY 12866
43.062262, -73.774350

Tioga Downs Casino Resort

2384 W River Road,
Nichols, NY 13812
42.023969, -76.413083

Turning Stone Resort Casino

Wicked Good Pizza
5218 Patrick Road,
Verona, NY 13478
43.115063, -75.589165

Vernon Downs Casino Hotel

4229 Stuhlman Road,
Vernon, NY 13476

Chapter # 05 – Erie Canal

Barge Canal

The Mohawk River, Tonawanda Creek, Pools Brook,

Oswego River, Seneca River, Genesee River, Clyde River and part of the Hudson River form the *'Barge'* Canal that in 1905 combined four main canals to form the Barge canal that opened in 1917-8; it replaced the *Erie Canal that was built from 1817 to 1825.*

The four existing canals were the *Erie Canal*, the *Oswego Canal*, the *Cayuga–Seneca Canal*, and the *Champlain Canal*.

Per Wikipedia

> "The Erie Canal connects the Hudson River to Lake Erie; the Cayuga–Seneca Canal connects Seneca Lake and Cayuga Lake to the Erie Canal; the Oswego Canal connects the Erie Canal to Lake Ontario; and the Champlain Canal connects the Hudson River to Lake Champlain."

The original Erie Canal was four (4) feet deep, 40 feet wide, and mostly hand-dug by the Irish and other laborers over the period of 1817 to 1825. The canal was 363 miles long and contained 83 lift locks. It proved so popular at the time as it cut nearly two weeks off of normal wagon travel that it became necessary to replace it with the Barge Canal that could handle bigger and bigger boats. The Barge Canal is 525-miles in length, but much wider and deeper, and is now considered to be the oldest public works transportation project still being used in the states.

The remains of the Old Erie Canal are at *Schoharie Crossing -Yankee Hill Lock 28*, Amsterdam, NY. (Shown) The majority of the locks and sites in this chapter are on the 'new and wider' 1905 Barge Canal that to many is considered to be the 'Erie Canal'. *(Picture is public domain, US NPS)*

This chapter provides the reader with locations of locks, parks, some trails, and some museums that are along, part of, or near the canals. The chapter is NOT all-inclusive, but may be the one of the most complete condensed description of the canals.

Amherst Veterans Canal Park

Buffalo, NY 14228
43.064818, -78.802817

Auriesville Pilgrimage Lunch Area

Boat launching area near the *Schoharie Crossing State Park*.

Queen Anne Road,

Amsterdam, NY 12010
42.953136, -74.238404

Barge Canal Lock at Genesee River (W)

421 Genesee Park Blvd,
Rochester, NY 14619
43.126189, -77.651168

Black Rock Lock

3 Dann Street,
Buffalo, NY 14207
42.935017, -78.907193

Canalway Trail – Old Erie Canal State Park

Oneida, NY 13421
43.105278, -75.681743

Canastota Canal Town Museum

122 Canal Street,
Canastota, NY 13032
43.079703, -75.751956

Cayuga-Seneca Canal, Taintor Gate Dam at Lock CS-4, Waterloo, Seneca County

Seneca Falls
New York 13148
42.914723, -76.786550

Champlain Canal, Lock C2, Town of Halfmoon, Saratoga County

15 1 Lock Road
North America
42.824247, -73.664338

Chittenango Landing Canal Boat Museum

717 Lakeport Road,
Chittenango, NY 13037
43.060022, -75.871352

East Guard Lock and Original Erie Canal Prism

This is the 1825 Clinton's Ditch version of the Erie Canal that was used to drain floodwaters away from the *Schoharie Crossing -Yankee Hill Lock 28*. Plan on 30 minutes.

Enlarged Erie Canal Lock 18 – Cohoes / Jacksonburg, Herkimer County

248 N Mohawk Street,
Cohoes, NY 12047
42.784761, -73.711549

Enlarged Erie Canal Lock 56

7473 Dry Dock Road,
Lyons, NY 14489
43.065902, -77.026397

Enlarged Erie Canal Lock 60

2574 Quaker Road,
Palmyra, NY 14522
43.070155, -77.282305

Erie Canal – Great Embankment Park

Marsh Road,
Pittsford, NY 14534
43.073156, -77.490952

Erie Canal 1st Bypass

13 Canal Street,
Sylvan Beach, NY 13157
43.195364, -75.729075

Erie Canal Boat Launch

426 Ayrault Road,
Fairport, NY 14450
43.079400, -77.459492

Erie Canal Discovery Center

24 Church Street,
Lockport, NY 14094
43.170946, -78.694833

Erie Canal Heritage Trail – Palmyra

Palmyra, NY 14522
New York
43.065282, -77.248761

Erie Canal Lock at Moss Island/Mohawk River

New York
43.038370, -74.846685

Erie Canal Lock at Plantation Island/Mohawk River

New York
43.016218, -74.916898

Erie Canal Museum

318 Erie Blvd E,
Syracuse, NY 13202
43.050682, -76.148830

Erie Canal Trail N. Canal Road Parking Spot - Lockport

7839 LA-57,
Lockport, NY 14094
43.186836, -78.666015

Erie Canal Village

Permanently Closed

Erie Canal Village
Fort Bull Road
Rome, NY 13440
43.225593, -75.502587

Erie Canalway National Heritage Corridor

The Erie Canal was built between 1817 and 1825 and this organization is helping to keep the history alive. Plan on 15 minutes.

Erie Canalway National Heritage Corridor
Oneida, NY 13421
43.078928, -75.639655

Erie Canalway Trail – Fort Plain

Fort Plain, NY 13339
42.938317, -74.623731

Erie Canalway Trail – Little Falls

Little Falls, NY 13365
43.037690, -74.845260

Erie Canalway Trail – Pendleton - Parking

6000-6174 E Canal Road,
Lockport, NY 14094
43.132448, -78.724911

Lockport Caves

5 Gooding Street,
Lockport, NY 14094
43.171935, -78.692303

Harbor Lock – Mohawk/Utica

E River Drive,
Mohawk, NY 13357

New York
43.117761, -75.228085

Harder Canal Park

Newark, NY 14513
43.052847, -77.127038

Limestone Creek Aqueduct, Old Erie Canal

New York
43.044061, -76.010531

Lock 01 – Aurelius

6817 River Road
Cayuga, New York 13034
42.948014, -76.734384

Lock 01 – Waterford/Hudson River

Champlain Canal Lock 1

15 Lock One Road,
Waterford, NY 12188
42.824245, -73.664339

Lock 02 – Waterford

Erie Canal Lock E-2
Waterford
New York 12188
42.789524, -73.682131

Lock 02 & 3 – Cayuga & Seneca Canal

These locks are on the *Van Cleef Lake* to the *Cayuga and Seneca Canal*, and are the Canal Corporation Locks 2 & 3. You can visit each while visiting the *Elizabeth Cady*

Stanton House on the next block. Plan on 30 minutes.

Van Cleef Lake
Seneca Falls, NY 13148
42.914697, -76.786646

Lock 03 – Waterford

New York 12188
42.794906, -73.686158

Lock 04 – Waterloo / Waterford, Saratoga County

Canal Corporation
50 Washington Street,
Waterloo, NY 13165
42.901043, -76.862998

Lock 05 – Waterford

New York 12188
42.802196, -73.696300

Lock 06 – Waterford

New York 12188
42.802898, -73.701811

State Canal Park – Lock 6

Lock 6 State Canal Park
Waterford, NY 12188
42.803694, -73.708057

Lock 07 – Niskayuna

Lock 7 Road,
Niskayuna, NY 12309
42.802881, -73.847100

Lock 7 Dam Overlook

Sugar Hill Road,
Rexford, NY 12148
42.808156, -73.842476

Lock 08 – Oswego/ Scotia

New York
43.456551, -76.508768

State Canal Park – Lock 8

Lock 8 State Canal Park
106 Rice Road,
Schenectady, NY 12306
42.828797, -73.991692

Lock 08 – Schenectady,

New York
42.829440, -73.991480

Lock 09 – Rotterdam / Schenectady

State Canal Park
Schenectady, NY 12302
42.879187, -74.040032

State Canal Park – Lock 9

Lock 9 State Canal Park
Schenectady, NY 12302
42.879208, -74.039934

Lock 10 – Amsterdam

New York
42.917142, -74.140869

Lock 11 – Amsterdam

366 W Main Street
Amsterdam, NY 12010
42.946449, -74.209708

Lock 12 – Fort Hunter

Fort Hunter, NY 12069
42.945623, -74.288519

Lock 13 – Fultonville

Fultonville, NY 12072
42.917702, -74.445651

Lock 14 – Palatine Bridge, Montgomery County

6 Spring Street
Palatine Bridge, NY 13428
42.909754, -74.577232

Lock 15 – Fort Plain

Otsuago Club Road
Fort Plain, NY 13339
42.938652, -74.622059

Lock 16 – Fort Plain

Mindenville Drive
Fort Plain, NY 13339
42.992297, -74.708578

Lock 17 – Little Falls/ Moss Island

Erie Canal Lock 17
Little Falls, NY 13365
43.038417, -74.846580

Lock 18 – Mohawk

Mohawk, NY 13407
43.016212, -74.916894

Lock 19 – Rexford / Clifton Park

Lock 19 of the Historic Erie Canal
Frankfort, NY 13340
43.073845, -75.113895

Vischer Ferry Nature & Historic Preserve

Pine Grove Lane,
Rexford, NY 12148

Clifton Park

New York 12148
42.786065, -73.820647

Lock 20 – Marcy

New York
43.142797, -75.291235

State Canal Park – Lock 20

Lock 20 State Canal Park
Marcy, NY 13403
43.142828, -75.290592

Lock 20 - Park Trailhead & Parking

5842 NY-291,
Marcy, NY 13403
43.145180, -75.296881

Lock 21 – Rome

7187-7155 Lock Road
Rome, NY 13440

43.208798, -75.618664

Lock 22 – Rome

3918-3998 Wood Creek Road
Rome, NY 13440
43.209531, -75.644902

Verona

New York
43.209832, -75.644887

Lock 23 – Brewerton

Brewerton, NY 13029
43.238759, -76.196870

Lock 23 State Canal Park

Brewerton, NY 13029
43.238759, -76.196870

Lock at Clay

County Route 33,
Pennellville, NY 13132

Lock 24 – Baldwinsville, Onondaga County

33 Water Street
Baldwinsville, NY 13027
43.155534, -76.333018

Lock 25 – Mays Point, Seneca County

Mays Point Road,
Seneca Falls, NY 13148
42.998786, -76.761789

Lock 26 – Clyde

11299 Lock Road,
Clyde, NY 14433
43.059017, -76.838423

Lock 27 – Lyons, Wayne County

95 Leach Road,
Lyons, NY 14489
43.062469, -76.996083

Lock 28 – Lyons

7499-7469 Dry Dock Road
Lyons, NY 14489
43.062481, -77.019842

Lock 28 – Schoharie Crossing -Yankee Hill

See the write-up on the Schoharie Crossing in this chapter.

Amsterdam, NY 12010
42.952780, -74.238978

Lock 28B – Newark

Erie Canal Lock 28B
106 N Clinton Street,

Newark, NY 14513
43.046744, -77.084278

Lock 29 – Palmyra Wayne County

Wayne County
New York 14522
43.065280, -77.248757

Lock 30 – Macedon

Erie Canal Heritage Trail,
Macedon, NY 14502
New York
43.073328, -77.301883

Lock 32 – Pittsford

Erie Canal Heritage Trail,
Pittsford, NY 14534
New York
43.091211, -77.544907

Lock 33 – Rochester

Canal Park
1159-1175 Edgewood Ave,
Rochester, NY 14618
43.096166, -77.568389

Lock 34 – Lockport Flight, Lockport, Niagara County

Pine Street
Lockport, NY 14094

43.170939, -78.692955

Lock 34? – Rochester,

Kendrick Road
Rochester, NY 14620
43.116942, -77.633462

Lock 35 – Lockport Flight, Lockport, Niagara County

Pine Street
Lockport, NY 14094
43.170939, -78.692955

Lock 60 – Palmyra

Enlarged Erie Canal Lock 60
2574 Quaker Road,
Palmyra, NY 14522
43.070155, -77.282298

Lockport Locks & Erie Canal Cruises

210 Market Street,
Lockport, NY 14094
43.175268, -78.687194

Mohawk Valley Gateway Overlook Pedestrian Bridge

1 Bridge Street,
Amsterdam, NY 12010
42.935322, -74.195411

Old Champlain Canal

Waterford, NY 12188
42.811236, -73.676828

Old Champlain Canal Lock 8

Halfmoon
New York 12118
42.869685, -73.687989

Old Champlain Canal Sidecut Locks

Waterford
New York 12188
42.790021, -73.681709

Old Champlain Canal Weighlock

Waterford
New York 12188
42.794259, -73.678907

Old Erie Canal Historic Park - Pools Brook

Kirkville, NY 13082
43.071604, -75.923786

Old Erie Canal State Historic Park - Cedar Bay

Canalway Trail- Old Erie Canal State Park,
East Syracuse, NY 13057
43.044298, -76.050901

Old Erie Canal State Historic Park – East Syracuse

Canalway Trail- Old Erie Canal State Park,
East Syracuse, NY 13057
43.043429, -76.020958

Old Erie Canal State Historic Park - Kirkville

Canalway Trail- Old Erie Canal State Park,
Kirkville, NY 13082
43.069703, -75.949831

Old Erie Canal State Historic Park - Minoa

Fayetteville, NY 13066
43.053896, -76.000535

Old Erie Canal State Park - Parking Area

Chittenango, NY 13037
43.060529, -75.870831

Oneida River Canal Lock 23

Brewerton, NY 13029
43.238815, -76.196379

Oswego Canal Lock 1

98 State Street
Phoenix, NY 13135
43.229466, -76.301499

Oswego Canal Lock 2

Fulton, NY 13069
43.316713, -76.414783

Oswego Canal Lock 3, Minetto, Oswego County

Fulton/ Granby, NY 13069
New York 13069
43.324279, -76.418637

Oswego Canal Lock 4

12-14 S 1st Street
Fulton, NY 13069
43.324316, -76.418669

Oswego Canal Lock 5

2796 NY-48
Oswego, NY 13126
43.400556, -76.473223

Oswego Canal Lock 6

New York
43.444180, -76.494301

Schoharie Crossing State Historic Site

Opens at 1 pm on Sunday, and is closed on Monday and Tuesday, this is an 1823 section of the Old Erie Canal where it crossed the Schoharie Creek via an aqueduct. There are locks and the remains of the Old Erie Canal nearby that you can view by taking short hikes along the paths. Locks 20, 28, and 29 are nearby. There is a small museum, and there are boat launching and picnic areas for your enjoyment.

The Aqueduct has been partly destroyed by the government due to it acting like a dam across the creek and causing local flooding. Other sections of the aqueduct have been failing, so it will eventually disappear. Plan on 30 minutes to see the area, several hours to explore the locks, old canal bed, and the area.

129 Schoharie Street,
Fort Hunter, NY 12069
42.938880, -74.281138

Old Erie Canal Aqueduct

New York
42.939542, -74.286340

NY Tribes Hill (Aqueduct) Boat Launch & Park

Dufel Road,
Amsterdam, NY 12010
42.938355, -74.289103

Seneca Falls River Locks

Cayuga and Seneca Canal

These locks are on the Van Cleef Lake to the *Cayuga and Seneca Canal*, and are the *Canal Corporation Locks 2 & 3*. You can visit each while visiting the *Elizabeth Cady Stanton House* on the next block. Plan on 30 minutes.

New York 13148
42.914690, -76.786609

State Boat Ramp – North Tonawanda

4682-, 4794 Tonawanda Creek Road,
North Tonawanda, NY 14120
43.065102, -78.802708

The Lockville Locks in Newark Marker

Newark, NY 14513
43.047268, -77.084245

The Old Erie Canal - Rochester

2681 Ridgeway
Ave,
Rochester, NY
14626
43.186110, -
77.708081

Tow Path Park

Hertel Ave,
Buffalo, NY 14207
42.939590, -78.908357

Widewaters Canal Park

5263 NY-31,
Newark, NY 14513
43.050417, -77.131126

Chapter # 06 – Historical & Heritage Societies

Historical Societies are usually run by volunteers that believe in their community and the preservation of the

history, historic buildings, and other sites that should not be destroyed by 'progress'. Some of these have or can suggest tours of their neighborhoods, some have tours that you can book, and some have museums that you can visit. Here are a few of the many in this area of New York State. *{Picture is the Tubman House}*

Arcade Historical Society

331 Main Street,
Arcade, NY 14009
42.534261, -78.426057

Avon Preservation & Historical Society

17 Genesee Street
Avon, NY 14414
42.911799, -77.746608

Big Springs Historical Society

Big Springs Historical Society

3095 Main Street
Caledonia, NY 14423
42.973849, -77.854970

Broome County Historical Society

Literacy Volunteers of Broome/ Tioga Counties
185 Court Street,
Binghamton, NY 13901
42.100280, -75.906532

Buffalo Fire Historical Society

Buffalo Fire Historical Society
1850 William Street,
Buffalo, NY 14206
42.884933, -78.802235

Cleveland Historical Society

8 North Street,
Cleveland, NY 13042
43.233966, -75.881534

East Bloomfield Historical Society

Historical Society
8 South Ave,
East Bloomfield, NY 14443
42.896240, -77.434713

Endicott History and Heritage Center

40 Washington Ave
Endicott, NY 13760

42.103301, -76.048582

Fly Creek Grange Hall / Historical Society

Fly Creek Grange Hall / Historical Society
212-216 Cemetery Road,
Fly Creek, NY 13337
42.716911, -74.983409

Friends of History In Fulton

177 S 1st Street,
Fulton, NY 13069
43.319297, -76.414971

Herkimer County Historical Society

Herkimer County Historical Society
406 N Main Street,
Herkimer, NY 13350
43.029481, -74.989379

Landmark Society of Western New York

Corn Hill Neighbors Association

This group provides tours of several buildings in the
general area, and is helping to save these historic
buildings.

Landmark Society of Western New York, Inc.
133 S Fitzhugh Street,
Rochester, NY 14608
43.150443, -77.612577

1840's Greek Revival House & Society HQ

Opens at 9:00 AM this is the society's home building.

Lima Historical Society

Lima Historical Society
1850 Rochester Street,
Lima, NY 14485
42.906871, -77.612368

Little Falls Historical Society & Museum

Little Falls Historical Society & Museum
319 S Ann Street,
Little Falls, NY 13365
43.042779, -74.859145

Madison County Historical Society

Madison County Historical Society
435 Main Street,
Oneida, NY 13421
43.087539, -75.646390

Manlius Historical Society

109 Pleasant Street,
Manlius, NY 13104
43.003220, -75.978921

NYS Equal Rights Heritage Center

NYS Equal Rights Heritage Center
25 South Street,

Auburn, NY 13021
42.929903, -76.566759

New York State Historical Association (NYSHA)

New York State Historical Association
80 Lake Street,
Cooperstown, NY 13326
42.716963, -74.928449

Ontario County Historical Society

Ontario County Historical Society
55 N Main St, Canandaigua, NY 14424
42.889929, -77.282398

Rome Historical Society & Museum

200 Church Street,
Rome, NY 13440
43.212215, -75.454632

Schenectady County Historical Society

1601, 32 Washington Ave,
Schenectady, NY 12305
42.817177, -73.949469

Schuyler County Historical Society

108 N Catherine Street,
Montour Falls, NY 14865
42.347737, -76.844847

Seneca Falls Historical Society

55 Cayuga Street,
Seneca Falls, NY 13148
42.915196, -76.794958

Chapter # 07
– Hiking Trails

Hiking, biking, and equestrian trails can be fun, interesting, a learning experience, and a means of exercise and just getting in touch with nature.

{Picture is from Wikipedia and is of the 9-mile creek trail, it is public domain}

The hiking trails of New York are varied and can be as short as a quarter mile, or as long as the state is wide, i.e. the *Erie Canal Trail*.

Provided are the names of the trails and the towns with GPS. Actual end points of many trails may be difficult to determine as each may start from another trail, or from unnamed roads. Thus, use the provided GPS to map out your hike in advance of doing the hike. Always hike in pairs or groups, or if alone let someone know where you are going and when you expect to return to your home base.

Always take water, sunscreen, and some communications device with you, if possible. Watch for wild animals, insects, and snakes on the more rural and wilderness trails; for strange characters on all trails. Take a camera and take lots of pictures; most trails have dozens of great photo opportunities. Enjoy!

Backbone Trail

Burdett, NY 14818
42.514088, -76.808653

Bear Trail

Ithaca, NY 14850
42.409928, -76.514122

Bear Trap Creek Bikeway

5113-5131 Ley Creek Drive,
Syracuse, NY 13211
43.087738, -76.163422

Burnt Hill Trail

Burdett, NY 14818
42.484395, -76.796224

Butternut Creek Trail

6852 Kinne Road,
Fayetteville, NY 13066
43.042211, -76.048625

Canalway Trail- Old Erie Canal State Park

Chittenango, NY 13037
43.060419, -75.870918

Cascadilla Gorge Trail

Walkway to the gorge & its waterfall

Cascadilla Gorge Trail
Ithaca, NY 14850
42.442907, -76.494038

Catherine Valley Trail (Bicycle Trail and Hiking)

265 N Catherine Street,
Montour Falls, NY 14865
42.350506, -76.851699

Enfield Lake Trail

Newfield, NY 14867
42.396703, -76.558648

Erie Canalway Trail

Little Falls, NY 13365
43.037690, -74.845260

Esker Brook Trail

Seneca Falls, NY 13148
42.974235, -76.783844

Finger Lakes Trail

Watkins Glen, NY 14891
42.374476, -76.871201

Fort Herkimer Rest Area & River Trail

Mohawk, NY 13407
43.018516, -74.960456

Geyser Creek Trail

19 Roosevelt Drive,
Saratoga Springs, NY 12866
43.051116, -73.805525

Gorge Trail

112 E Buttermilk Falls Road,
Ithaca, NY 14850
42.416308, -76.521347

Grasslands Trail

Henrietta, NY 14467
43.023954, -77.574381

Great Flats Nature Trail

W Campbell Road,
Schenectady, NY 12306
42.813796, -73.982006

Green Lakes Perimeter Trail

7673-7581, NY-290,
Kirkville, NY 13082
43.054231, -75.997225

Indian Trail

Watkins Glen, NY 14891
42.374602, -76.875019

Interloken Trail Parking Lot

2375-2371 Town Line Road,
Interlaken, NY 14847
42.543940, -76.799637

Jesse Kregal Pathway

Japanese Garden,
1 Museum Court,
Buffalo, NY 14216
42.935351, -78.875454

Kane Mountain Hiking Trail

290-294 Green Lake Rd,
Caroga Lake, NY 12032
43.180214, -74.504503

Labrador Hollow Unique Area (Trail)

Labrador Road,
Tully, NY 13159
42.792578, -76.052174

Lake Treman Trail

Ithaca, NY 14850
42.395179, -76.508541

Lakeshore Trail

Barker, NY 14012
43.374268, -78.483471

Lindsay-Parsons Biodiversity Preserve Trail

2521 Spencer Road,
Spencer, NY 14883
42.307250, -76.521050

Ludovico Sculpture Trail

Seneca Falls, NY 13148
42.908868, -76.801049

Mill Island Trail

The Point on Mill Island Trail
17 Marble Street,
Baldwinsville, NY 13027
43.156172, -76.329521

Mohawk Hudson Bikeway Parking

East Street,
Schenectady, NY 12309
42.848129, -73.888520

Mohawk Hudson Hike Bike Trail

Albany, NY 12202
42.642015, -73.750999

Mohawk River Trail

Rome, NY 13440
43.209875, -75.449396

Monkey Run, Cayuga Trail

Ithaca, NY 14850
42.455960, -76.451047

Moyer Creek Hiking Trail

Frankfort, NY 13340
43.036573, -75.074735

Natty Bumpo's Cave Hike

315-309, Co Rd 31,
Cooperstown, NY 13326
42.712519, -74.911281

Olmsted's RiverWalk Garden

Buffalo, NY 14207
42.957105, -78.910695

Alexander Petofi Bust at Riverside Park

Buffalo, NY 14207
42.957355, -78.909322

Hasek's Heroes

2607 Niagara Street,
Buffalo, NY 14207
42.955500, -78.909443

Oneida Indian Nation Trail

Oneida, NY 13421
43.088127, -75.667750

Oneida Rail Trail

Oneida, NY 13421
43.082459, -75.693637

Onondaga Trail Lewiston

101-175 N 2nd Street,
Lewiston, NY 14092
43.174451, -79.046579

Peak #1 Loop Trailhead

Town Hwy,
Waterville, NY 13480
42.919420, -75.304790

Pipeline Trail

Vestal, NY 13850
42.083420, -75.961093

Rapids High Hiking Trail (Cliff Base)

1 Depot Ave W,
Niagara Falls, NY 14305
43.110711, -79.056898

Ravine Trail

Vestal, NY 13850
42.080809, -75.960495

Rim Trail

Ithaca, NY 14850
42.417148, -76.520894

Russell Park Mountain Biking Trails

Ilion, NY 13357
43.003592, -75.030132

S Rim Trail

Watkins Glen, NY 14891
42.373081, -76.880485

Seneca Trail

Seneca Falls, NY 13148
42.967530, -76.739839

Silver Lake Outlet Trail

Perry, NY 14530
42.716509, -78.014715

Sleeping Lion Hiking Trail

Cooperstown, NY 13326
42.793217, -74.876909

South Spring Pool Trail

3395 Hwy 20,
Seneca Falls, NY 13148
42.970565, -76.771462

Spencer Crest Hiking Trails

This is a series of interconnecting trails that cover some 250 acres of wooded land. There is a pond, an observatory, a planetarium, and a main building / museum / classroom area. The following are the names of the various interconnecting trails; map out your hike before attempting this maze.

Dike Way, Maples Run, Ski Slope Trail, Laurel Lane, Blue Bird Path, Deer Run, Overlook Pass, High Meadow Trail, Ridge Run, College Way, Hemlock Pass, Eileen

Corning, NY 14830
42.116188, -77.082220

Collins Observatory

Academic Drive,
Corning, NY 14830
42.118094, -77.077709

Planetarium

Corning, NY 14830
42.118019, -77.076369

Tinker Falls

Tinker Falls Trail,
Tully, NY 13159
42.782571, -76.033135

Tinker's Falls Accessible Trail Parking

Tinker Falls Trail,
Tully, NY 13159
42.780055, -76.035744

Tinker Park Nature Trail

Pittsford, NY 14534
43.067520, -77.574517

Trailhead Niagara Gorge Hiking Trail

Niagara Falls, NY 14303
43.094789, -79.061693

Unnamed Road

Oneida, NY 13421
43.091600, -75.661315

Vestal Rail Trail

196 Stage Road #156,
Vestal, NY 13850

42.088083, -76.050846

Vroman's Nose Hiking Trail

264 Mill Valley Road,
Middleburgh, NY 12122
42.594711, -74.358293

Watkins Glen Gorge Trail

971 N Franklin Street,
Watkins Glen, NY 14891
42.375068, -76.873333

Chapter # 08 – Lighthouses

New York State in on Lake Erie & Lake Ontario {Two

of the Great Lakes} and there is much shipping in the area, thus there are several lighthouses along the lake's shores. Here are some of the NYS lighthouses that you may want to visit or obtains photos of while you tour the areas. ·

{This is the Salmon River (Selkirk (Port Ontario) Light). Picture is from Wikipedia and is public

domain}

Barcelona Lighthouse

East Lake Road,
Westfield, NY 14787
42.341100, -79.594837

Braddock Point Light

Hilton, NY 14468
43.341171, -77.761922

Charlotte Genesee Lighthouse

70 Lighthouse Street,
Rochester, NY 14612
43.252831, -77.610741

Dunkirk Lighthouse

1 Point Drive N,
Dunkirk, NY 14048
42.493893, -79.353947

Old Fort Niagara Light, Youngstown, NY

Fort Niagara State Park,
Scott Ave,
Youngstown, NY 14174
43.261755, -79.060524

Oak Orchard Lighthouse

14357 Ontario Street,
Kent, NY 14477
43.372311, -78.191495

Salmon River Lighthouse & Marina

5 Lake Road Extension,
Pulaski, NY 13142
43.574600, -76.202309

Thirty Mile Point Lighthouse

Barker, NY 14012
43.374946, -78.485951

Tibbetts Point Lighthouse

33435 County Road 6,
Cape Vincent, NY 13618
44.100647, -76.370034

Verona Beach Lighthouse Association

2454 4th Ave,
Verona Beach, NY 13162
43.189324, -75.731017

West Pierhead Lighthouse

Lake Ontario
43.473244, -76.516719

Chapter # 09 – Memorials & Monuments

 Memorials & Monuments are usually plaques or statues that are in town squares or public parks and you can plan on having to find a parking spot, and then some 5 minutes or so reading and taking pictures.

American Civil War Memorial

Waterloo
New York 13165
42.901711, -76.863153

Frederick Douglass Monument

Frederick Douglass Monument
Rochester, NY 14607
43.153566, -77.605160

DeWitt 9/11 Memorial Monument

5400 Butternut Drive,
East Syracuse, NY 13057
43.046187, -76.050140

General Herkimer Monument

Herkimer, NY 13350
43.025345, -74.989720

Fort Stanwix National Monument

100 N James Street,
Rome, NY 13440
43.210564, -75.455270

Joan and Victor Fuzak Memorial Garden

329 Erie Street,
Buffalo, NY 14202
42.878854, -78.887236

New Hartford Veterans Memorial

New Hartford Veteran Memorial
11 Evalon Road,
New Hartford, NY 13413
43.076183, -75.307172

Veteran's Memorial Park

N James Street,
Rome, NY 13440
43.212973, -75.455962

Chapter # 10 – Military Parks & Forts

The history of New York State goes back to the time of the Mayflower and the settlers from England.

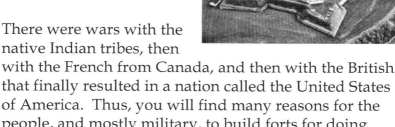

{Picture is from NYS Parks, and is of the Fort Ontario State Historic Site}

There were wars with the native Indian tribes, then with the French from Canada, and then with the British that finally resulted in a nation called the United States of America. Thus, you will find many reasons for the people, and mostly military, to build forts for doing battle, protecting assets, or used as supply depots. Here are some of the old forts that dotted the region.

Fort Brewerton

Oliver Stevens Blockhouse Museum

This two-story log blockhouse houses artifacts of the area that date back some 10,000 years or more. It is open the third Saturday of each month, April through December, 12-noon to 4pm. Plan on 45 minutes or more.

9 US-11,
Central Square, NY 13036
43.241820, -76.141160

Buffalo Naval Park

On display and open for self-touring are the Cleveland-class cruiser *USS Little Rock*, the Fletcher-class destroyer *USS The Sullivans*, and the submarine *USS Croaker*. There are also several other smaller vessels and there are a museum and other buildings to explore. Plan on three hours or more.

Buffalo Naval Park
Military Park 1 Naval Park Cove
Buffalo, NY 14202
42.877811, -78.879127

Fort Bull

Fort Wood Creek

This 1750s fort seemed to be a bad luck fortress as the French and the Indians burned it to the ground. For *Fort Wood Creek* was built on the site to replace it, but it too was totally destroyed. Plan on 20 minutes. The loss of the fort disrupted the supply lines to *Fort Oswego* and nearly caused its demise.

Rome, NY 13440
43.223720, -75.502119

Fort Herkimer Church

This 1753 church is not open to the public unless you make prior arrangements, but you can walk the grounds and marvel in the construction that allows it to be the only remaining building of Fort Herkimer. The church has a history during the French and Indian War and the 1775 American Revolutionary War period. Plan on 15 to 30 minutes.

575 NY-5S,
Mohawk, NY 13407
43.018060, -74.954051

Fort Klock Restoration

Open Friday, Saturday, and Sunday. This private property is considered a 'fort' but is actually a 'fortified' farm and homestead that was built by *Johannes Klock*, 1750, a German Palatine who came to the area with the great Palatine migration. Plan on 45 minutes to an hour.

7214 NY-5,
St Johnsville, NY 13452
42.985541, -74.648855

Fort Ontario State Historic Site

Fort Oswego

This popular tourist destination is on the lake and provides great views from its five-point 'Star' shaped fortified walls. Check the NYS official website for opening dates and time, each may change depending on the month.

Per the NYS Park Service website

"The fourth and current Fort Ontario is built on the ruins of three earlier fortifications dating to the French and Indian War, Revolutionary War, and War of 1812. It was occupied by the U.S. Army through World War II. From 1944 to 1946 the fort served as the only refugee camp in the United States for mostly Jewish victims of the Nazi Holocaust under an Executive Order from President Franklin D. Roosevelt. A post cemetery containing the graves of 77 officers, soldiers, women, and children who served at Fort Ontario in war and peace is situated on the grounds, which are open year-round from dawn to dusk.

In 1946 Fort Ontario was transferred to the State of New York and housed World War II veterans and their families until 1953. It opened as a state historic site in 1953."

1 E 4th Street,
Oswego, NY 13126
43.465836, -76.508209

Fort Plain Museum & Historical Park

Fort Rensselaer

Closed on Mondays and Tuesdays this fort was used to defend the citizens of the area in the 1779 era and in 1780 *General Van Rensselaer* commandeered the fort and renamed it *Fort Rensselaer* after himself. The fort served it purpose for several years and is now a museum that you can visit. Plan on two hours or more.

Fort Plain Museum & Historical Park
1160, 389 Canal Street,
Fort Plain, NY 13339
42.940148, -74.630206

Fort Niagara

Fort Niagara State Park

Fort Niagara Lighthouse

From the official oldfortniagara.org website

"The three flags flown daily above the parade ground symbolize the nations which have held Fort Niagara. Each competed for the support of a fourth nation: the powerful Iroquois Confederacy. The French established the first post here, **Fort Conti**, in 1679. Its successor, **Fort Denonville** (1687-88) was equally short lived. In 1726 France finally erected a permanent fortification with the construction of the impressive **"French Castle."** Britain gained control of **Fort Niagara** in 1759, during the French & Indian War, after a nineteen-day siege. The British held the post throughout the American Revolution but were forced, by treaty, to yield it to the United States in 1796. Fort Niagara was recaptured by the British in 1813. It was ceded to the United States a second time in 1815 at the end of the War of 1812."

Plan on four or more hours to explore the park, the fort, the lighthouse, and the pathways.

Old Fort Niagara
102 Morrow Plaza,
Youngstown, NY 14174
43.262371, -79.060635

Fort Tompkins (Buffalo, New York)

Fort Adams

From the military.wikia.org website

"Fort Tompkins is a former fort in Buffalo, New York, overlooking the Niagara River. Built in August 1812 on top of the bluff at the bend of Niagara Street. Large earthwork mounting seven guns, and was the largest of eight batteries erected that summer. Also called Fort Adams. To the South was Old Sow Battery, and to the North was Gibson's Battery. British attacked Black Rock July 1813 and destroyed the Black Rock Blockhouse and spiked or carried off the guns at Fort Tompkins. It later became to the location of street railway barns in 1914.

There are no remains and perhaps not even a Historic Marker. Approximate location is:

Black Rock
Buffalo, NY
42.932522, -78.898679

Fort Porter

This fort dates back to the 1841 period and there were several buildings, but unfortunately private investors purchased the property and destroyed each. Today only a parking area and a statue remains. Plan on 10 minutes.

Fort Porter
952 Busti Ave,
Buffalo, NY 14213
42.901001, -78.898254

Military History Society of Rochester

Open Thursday, Friday, and Saturday this museum features the history of our military with emphasis on *Pearl Harbor* and the ships and aircraft of the attack. Plan on one hour.

Military History Society of Rochester
250 Goodman Street North 2nd Floor, 201,
Rochester, NY 14607
43.158146, -77.584639

Old Fort Erie

On the Canadian side of the Niagara River stands this War of 1812 fort and museum. Plan on one to two hours. Be sure to bring your passport as you will need it for your return to the US.

Old Fort Erie
350 Lakeshore Road,
Fort Erie, ON L2A 1B1, Canada
42.894642, -78.923931

Old Fort Niagara

Fort Niagara State Park

See Fort Niagara write-up

102 Morrow Plaza,
Youngstown, NY 14174
43.262369, -79.060635

Old Stone Fort Museum

This 'fort' was actually a 1772 church that was fortified and surrounded with fencing to ward off the enemy in 1780 when the British attacked it. The museum today includes a 1830s law office, a 1780s Dutch Barn, a 1700s home, and an 1890s one-room schoolhouse. Plan on two to four hours.

Old Stone Fort Museum
145 Fort Road,
Schoharie, NY 12157
42.677327, -74.301934

War of 1812 Bicentennial Peace Garden

This is a small roadside garden with a monument. Plan on 5 minutes.

117-123 W Main Street,
Batavia, NY 14020
42.999235, -78.190348

Chapter # 11 – Museums

New York State was one of the first states settled by those courageous folk from Europe and beyond, and thus there is much history that dates back into the 1600's. There were and still are many Native Indian Tribes that were in the territory long before the 'White Man', and they too have history to be told. Over the years of settlement, the state grew and there were many industries that sprung up, some of which are still active, many of which have been long obsolete or have moved to other locations.

This adds up to a diverse, interesting, and entertaining state that loves its history (I Love NY is its slogan), and thus dozens of attractions and museums. Here is a listing of many, not all, the museums in the area that you may find of interest.

Listed Alphabetically.

1840's Greek Revival House & Society HQ

See *Landmark Society of Western New York.*

1890 House Museum

Closed Sunday, Monday, Tuesday, and Wednesday this 1890 House Museum building looks like an ancient castle on the outside, and like a magnificent manor on the inside. The owner at the time was Industrialist *Chester F. Wickwire* (1843–1910) who had several inventions, and was a leader in the distribution of *Woven Wire* products worldwide. The house is said to be haunted, and thus there are several opportunities to *'hunt ghost'* while visiting, day or night. Plan on one to two hours.

37 Tompkins Street,
Cortland, NY 13045
42.596051, -76.182114

Albright-Knox Art Gallery

Closed on Monday this *'art'* gallery is loaded with artworks that may have been created by those that may have been *'slightly high'* at the time. You are in for a treat when you spend a few hours and lots of film or pixels visiting this unique gallery.

Albright-Knox Art Gallery
1285 Elmwood Ave,
Buffalo, NY 14222
42.932464, -78.875616

All Things Oz Museum

Open Saturday afternoons this museum is basically a collection of the toys, pictures, outfits, and such that were either used in the making of the *Wizard of Oz*, or were sold as Wizard of Oz keepsakes. Plan on one hour.

219 Genesee Street,
Chittenango, NY 13037
43.044945, -75.866930

Anonymous Arts Museum

What can one say; this repurposed church holds artwork from anonymous artists. Plan on 15 minutes.

Anonymous Arts Museum
606 Charlotte Valley Road,
Charlotteville, NY 12036
42.544707, -74.668996

Arkell Museum

Closed on Monday and opens late on Saturday and Sunday this museum features the Mohawk Valley and its history.

From the official website

"Bartlett Arkell, the first president of the **Beech-Nut Packing Company** founded the Canajoharie Library for the people of the village of Canajoharie. When it opened, gracing its walls were a dozen paintings from Arkell's personal collection, including works by **Gilbert Stuart and Robert Henri**. The paintings were so well received that in 1927, Arkell broke ground on our original museum building, and we became the Canajoharie Library and Art Gallery."

"The American painting collection includes seven oil paintings by **Winslow Homer** and significant paintings by many distinguished artists including; **Thomas Benton, William M. Chase, Childe Hassam, John Singer Sargent, Albert Bierstadt, and Gilbert Stuart**. Permanent and changing exhibitions also feature selections from the museum's Mohawk Valley History collection as well as the Beech-Nut collection of early twentieth-century advertising material."

Plan on two or more hours.

Arkell Museum
2 Erie Blvd,
Canajoharie, NY 13317
42.907388, -74.572093

Artmuseumofrochester

With a name like this, what can you expect when you visit what appears to be a private home that is open on Saturday and Sunday after 5 PM, so you can view some local artist works. Plan on 20 minutes.

Artmuseumofrochester
610 Monroe Ave,
Rochester, NY 14607
43.145334, -77.590989

Binghamton University Art Museum

Closed on Sunday and Monday and opens at noon on all other days of the week. This art museum has over 4,000 items that date back some 5,000 years shown in several galleries. Plan on two hours.

Binghamton University Art Museum
4400 Vestal Pkwy E,
Binghamton, NY 13901
42.088703, -75.968108

Brick Tavern Museum -Schuyler County Historical Society

Closed on Saturday, Sunday, and Monday this 1828 building and museum has items you may have never seen before. The author has been to many areas of the world and thought he could not see anything new, but this facility proved him incorrect, will it prove you wrong? Spend a few hours and see for yourself.

108 N Catherine Street,

Montour Falls, NY 14865
42.347719, -76.844856

Buffalo Museum of Science

The name says it all, this is a Science Museum that spans several venues and to make if more fun and interesting, it has lots of hands-on activities for the children and the child in you. Plan on two to four hours.

Buffalo Museum of Science
1020 Humboldt Pkwy,
Buffalo, NY 14211
42.906280, -78.843418

Buffalo Transportation Pierce Arrow Museum

Closed on Monday, Tuesday, and Wednesday this museum is a collection of the famous *Pierce Arrow automobiles* of the 1901 to 1938 era. The museum also has bikes, other unique vehicles, and a 1920's replica of a *Gas Station* that was designed by *Frank Lloyd Wright*. Plan on one to two hours or more.

See author's book on Tucson, Arizona for the Franklin Auto museum.

Buffalo Transportation Pierce Arrow Museum
263 Michigan Ave,
Buffalo, NY 14203
42.879112, -78.869464

Bundy Museum of History and Art

Closed on Sunday and Monday this museum contains items that represent the history of Binghamton, NY. You may see items like those from a 1930s barbershop, an old jukebox, antique clocks, etc. Plan on one hour.

129 Main Street
Binghamton, NY 13905
42.101644, -75.927913

Burchfield Penney Art Center

Closed on Mondays the art center features oil paintings from the 1800s to the present. Many are from local artist, some from internationally known artists. There is a gift shop and a small café for those that get hungry. Plan on one or more hours.

Burchfield Penney Art Center
1300 Elmwood Ave,
Buffalo, NY 14222
42.931534, -78.878408

Children's Museum of Oswego (CMOO)

This is a typical children's museum that caters to those between 3 and 10 years of age. It has been closed but claims to be open in June of 2019 after the renovations are completed. Plan on one or more hours.

7 W Bridge Street,
Oswego, NY 13126
43.456842, -76.510982

Corning Museum of Glass

If you like glass from 3,500 years ago, from our space telescopes, from Egyptian history, from just about every glass technology created, then Corning Glass is the place to visit. If you like, you can watch or take glass blowing classes, have a meal in their café, or do some shopping in the gift shop.

Plan on two to four plus hours.

1 Museum Way,
Corning, NY 14830
42.149823, -77.054208

Corning Museum of Glass Welcome Center

121 Center Way,
Corning, NY 14830
42.152595, -77.054121

Curtiss Wright Museum

This museum has antique motorcycles, vehicles, boats, and a big selection of Curtiss Wright aircraft for which they are known.
From the official website.

"Glenn Curtiss began his career as a builder of bicycles and then, motorcycles. In 1907 he became the "fastest man on earth" when he attained a speed of 136.4 MPH on his V8 powered motorcycle. An exact reproduction of this bike is one of several Curtiss motorcycles that are on display. On July 4th, 1908, Curtiss gained notoriety of a different kind when he flew his flying machine, named the **"June Bug"**, a distance of over 5000 feet to win the Scientific American Trophy. This was the first pre-announced, public flight in America - a feat that earned him **pilot's license # 1**. A full-sized reproduction of the "June Bug" is one of several historic aircraft on display.

Glenn Curtiss won world recognition as an aircraft builder and pilot in 1909 when he won the Gordon Bennett Trophy for speed at the First International Aviation Meet held in Reims, France"

Plan on two to three hours.

Glenn H Curtiss Museum
8419 NY-54,
Hammondsport, NY 14840
42.398721, -77.232926

Dansville Artworks

Closed Sunday, Monday, Tuesday, and Wednesday. This facility has local art on display and an area for consignment artists to display their work that is for sale to the general public. Plan on 45 minutes.

Dansville Artworks
153 Main Street,
Dansville, NY 14437
42.560118, -77.695429

Dr Best House and Medical Exhibit

Open on Saturdays only this museum has hundreds of items from 1884 to 1991 on display. Plan on one or more hours.

Dr Best House and Medical Exhibit
1568 Clauverwie Road,
Middleburgh, NY 12122
42.596230, -74.332928

Empire State Aerosciences Museum

Open Friday, Saturday, and Sunday this museum has an extensive collection of aircraft and ship models housed in an aircraft hanger. Plan on two to four hours.

250 Rudy Chase Drive
Glenville, NY 12302
42.860311, -73.932332

Everson Museum of Art

Closed on Monday and Tuesday. This somewhat 'way-out-there' art museum features many different types of artistic items; it also has one of the most extensive displays of ceramics and pottery in the US. Plan on two or more hours.

Everson Museum of Art
401 Harrison Street,
Syracuse, NY 13202
43.044735, -76.146740

Fairport Historical Museum

Bushnell's Basin Cemetery Tour

Limited hours, see their website. This is a 'different'
type of museum in that it has very limited hours, but
offers over a dozen tours to various homes and other
interesting buildings in the Fairport area. Plan on 45
minutes in the museum, hours on the tours.

18 Perrin Street,
Fairport, NY 14450
43.100376, -77.444244

Fenimore Art Museum

Open daily, this 1930s neo-Georgian mansion with
beautiful grounds overlooking the placid blue Otsego
lake houses many pieces of fine art and Native
American artifacts. Plan on two or more hours.

Fenimore Art Museum
5798 NY-80,
Cooperstown, NY 13326
42.715776, -74.927097

Genesee Country Village & Museum

Closed on Mondays this village is large and contains buildings from the Erie / Finger Lakes area towns that have been salvaged and moved to this location. You will enjoy spending a full day walking the paths and visiting all the buildings while talking to the folks that are reenacting the 1800s in the Genesee Valley. This is the third-largest collection of buildings and artifacts, some 20,000+, in the US and should be on your 'Bucket List' of places to visit in this part of NYS. Plan on a full 8-hour day; wear good walking shoes, bring water and suntan lotion, and the kids.

Genesee County Village & Museum
6108 E Lake Road,
Burt, NY 14028

George Eastman Museum

Closed on Monday the George Eastman museum rivals the Rockefellers in affluence due to his *Kodak* empire fortune. The museum is elaborate as are the surrounding gardens and grounds, so plan on two to four-hours minimum.

George Eastman Museum
900 East Ave,
Rochester, NY 14607
43.152838, -77.580078

H. Lee White Maritime Museum

Open afternoons from one to five. This maritime museum is on the pier at the Port of Oswego where the Oswego River enters Lake Ontario. It is close to the *West Pierhead Lighthouse* that sits out in the lake. You can visit a WWII D-day tugboat, and a wooden hull boat that you may get to take a ride in, if you are inclined. Plan on two or more hours.

1 E 1st Street
Oswego, NY 13126
43.464381, -76.515606

Maritime Museum Lot

1 W 1st Street,
Oswego, NY 13126
43.464584, -76.515859

Heroes of Baseball Wax Museum

Open daily this museum has full-size wax figures of baseball players from our sports history; you will see people like *Babe Ruth, Lou Gehrig, Pete Rose, Rickey Henderson,* and many others. Plan on one hour.

Heroes of Baseball Wax Museum
99 Main Street
Cooperstown, New York 13326
42.700441, -74.925167

Holland Land Office Museum

Closed on Sunday and Monday. This museum has Batavia history and a gift shop. The city of Batavia was founded in 1801 and this building was the Land Office where surveys and permits were obtained. There is a kitchen, office, and other rooms and items from the early 1800s. Plan on one hour.

131 W Main Street,
Batavia, NY 14020
42.999199, -78.190804

Hyde Hall Museum

Hyde Hall Covered Bridge

Glimmerglass State Park

Open daily this 1800 mansion is now a museum located on the shore of Lake Otsego; it has both downstairs and upstairs tours, as well as nighttime *'Ghost'* type tours. Be sure to stop at the *Hyde Hall Covered Bridge* and at *'Tin top'* the visitor's center for entry tickets. Plan on three or more hours.

267 Glimmerglass State Park
Cooperstown, NY 13326
42.793419, -74.873236

Irish American Heritage Museum

Closed on Monday and Tuesdays this museum features the history of the Irish that helped establish the area and the canal systems. There is an entire section on the *Irish Famine* of 1845-1853 and how it affected Ireland and the migration to the US. Plan on one or more hours.

370 Broadway,
Albany, NY 12207
42.647360, -73.750612

Iron Island Museum

Open Thursday night, and during the day on Friday and Saturday. The museum offers overnight 'Ghost' tours, which is fine considering that the museum is in a church's funeral home. Plan on several hours.

Iron Island Preservation Society
998 E Lovejoy Street,
Buffalo, NY 14206
42.890030, -78.811410

Iroquois Indian Museum

Opens at noon on Sunday and is closed on Monday. This museum is housed in a unique building that represents the '*Longhouses*' of some 400 years distant. The museum tells a thousand year history of the natives to area and it includes provisions for expansion and a deck for speakers and native dancing. Plan on one or more hours.

Iroquois Indian Museum
324 Caverns Road,
Howes Cave, NY 12092
42.691579, -74.407970

Liverpool Historian Museum

Liverpool Willow Museum

Open Thursday and Saturday the main museum features artifacts of the townspeople of Liverpool, NY. On the grounds is a separate building, the *Willow Museum*, which features willow weaving and its products and history. Their website has over 1,000 pictures of woven willow products. Plan on one hour or more.

314 2nd Street,
Liverpool, NY 13088
43.103917, -76.209170

Livingston County Historical

The 1890 Willard Hose House

The museum is housed in the cobblestone 1838 schoolhouse and on the grounds is the *Willard Hose House* that was once used for fire fighting equipment storage. The main museum was established to document and tell the history of Livingston County and its various towns. Plan on one hour or more.

Livingston County Historical Society
30 Center Street,
Geneseo, NY 14454
42.795441, -77.813230

Livonia Area Preservation Museum

This is a small strip mall type museum. Plan on 45 minutes.

Livonia Area Preservation

10 Commercial Street,
Livonia, NY 14487
42.821489, -77.669072

Long Homestead Historical Museum

Benjamin Long Homestead

Open Sunday afternoon, there are two parts to this facility, the first is the Homestead and the second is the museum housed in an old 1886 New York Central Railroad's Tonawanda Station. {Open Wednesdays, Thursdays, and Saturdays.}

Mr. Long and family settled here in 1828 alongside the Erie Canal and he and a small group of farmers, family men, businessmen, and politicians established the town of Tonawanda. The unique part of this museum, other than the 1810 to 1860 furnishings is the materials used to build it. The exterior is Cedar, and the interior is Black Walnut and White Oak; all of which were hand-cut at the site. Plan on one hour.

24 E Niagara Street
Tonawanda, NY 14150
43.021034, -78.875840

Lost World Museum

If you believe in creationism then this is the museum you should be seeking. Plan on one hour.

75 State Street
Phoenix, NY 13135
43.228816, -76.300212

Memorial Art Gallery

Closed on Monday and Tuesday this art gallery has three floors of permanent and rotating inventory including works from Grand Masters. On special days you can hear the Pipe Organ being played. Plan on two or more hours.

Memorial Art Gallery
500 University Ave,
Rochester, NY 14607
43.157746, -77.588145

miSci - Museum of Innovation and Science

Closed on Mondays this museum has dinosaurs, butterflies, a model railroad, nanotubes, space age items, and dozens of scientific displays. Plan on two hours or more.

15 Nott Terrace Heights
Schenectady, NY 12308
42.811831, -73.933719

Mount Morris Dam & Museum

William B. Hoyt II Visitor Center

This is a dam across the Genesee River where you can have a picnic, take a mile long hike, or take a tour into the bowels of a working dam. The dam was built in the 1948 to 1952 period to stop flooding and associated damages to the city of Rochester. It is one of the largest concrete dams in the nation. Plan on one to two hours.

William B. Hoyt II Visitor Center
6103 Visitor Center Road
Mt Morris, NY 14510

Munson-Williams-Proctor Arts Institute

Fountain Elms

Philip Johnson Building

Opens late on Sunday, closed on Mondays. There are two buildings in the art school complex, and *Fountain Elms* was the first converted to a museum in 1936; since then the Philip Johnson Building was added in 1955 and opened in 1960. The Fountain Elms building is a Victorian Style building; a Museum Education Wing that opened in 1995 connects it to the Philip Johnson Building. There are also sculpture garden, café, and gift shop areas. Plan on two or more hours.

Munson-Williams-Proctor Arts Institute
310 Genesee Street,
Utica, NY 13502
43.097572, -75.240168

Museum of Intrigue

Extended hours on Saturday and Sunday, opens at 1 pm on the other weekdays. Ok, you have been to all sorts of museums and are getting tired of 'seeking' history and all that 'boring' stuff, and then you find this place. Yes, it is sort of a museum, but it is also sort of a mystery house as it has *'Escape'* rooms and *'Puzzles'* or *'Stories'* that you have to solve, individually or as a group. There are nearly 30 storybook adventures that range from 20 minutes to an hour in length, you select and then follow the storyline and solve the story's mystery while learning about all the historic items in the museum.

306 Hiawatha Blvd W m302,
Syracuse, NY 13290
43.069321, -76.171532

Museum of Science & Technology

Closed on Mondays and Tuesdays. This museum is
said to have everything from dinosaurs to space travel
for your enjoyment. There is an IMAX Theater, a
planetarium, climbing wall, flight simulator and much
more for 'children' of all ages from 5 to 105. Plan on
two or more hours.

500 S Franklin Street,
Syracuse, NY 13202
43.047123, -76.155595

National Baseball Hall of Fame and Museum

Open daily this museum has some 38,000 items that have to do
with the last 100 years of the sport of baseball and its best players.
Plan on two to three hours.

PS, also try to visit the *baseball wax museum* that is a few blocks
distant.

National Baseball Hall of Fame and Museum
25 Main Street
Cooperstown, NY 13326
42.699941, -74.923215

National Museum of Dance & Hall of Fame

Closed on Monday this museum is housed in an old bathhouse and has several short movies, lots of items of dance, and a ton of history on all sorts of dance routines. Plan on one to two hours.

99 S Broadway,
Saratoga Springs, NY 12866
43.066128, -73.790200

National Museum of Play

The Strong Museum

This museum is difficult to miss due to its exterior design of colored blocks in a pile. Inside on the first floor you will find lots for the younger children to do; the second floor is for teens and adults. In total there are some 100,000 square feet of things to do, so plan on two or more hours.

The Strong Museum
1 Manhattan Square Drive,
Rochester, NY 14607
43.153028, -77.600870

National Toy Hall of Fame

See the write-up on the Strong Museum/ National Museum of Play.

New York 14607
43.152283, -77.601744

National Warplane Museum

Open on Saturdays and Mondays this indoor/outdoor museum has a dozen or so propeller type aircraft from past wars. It also provides *'rides'* for a fee. Plan on one hour.

3489 Big Tree Lane
Geneseo, NY 14454
42.796160, -77.846410

Niagara Wax Museum of History

Open daily this was museum has full-size figures of people that settled the area, saw the falls before anyone else, and some of those that dared to ride a barrel over the falls. There are also *Mark Twain* and *Abe Lincoln* as well as other characters from history. Plan on one hour.

303 Prospect Street,
Niagara Falls, NY 14303
43.086327, -79.064514

Oneida County History Center & Museum

Closed on Saturday and Sunday. This history center has tens of thousands of photos, documents, and artifacts that spell out the history of the county and its people. Plan on 30 minutes if not looking for something, hours if doing so.

1608 Genesee Street
Utica, NY 13502
43.091495, -75.252365

Palatine House 1743 Museum

Middleburgh and Schoharie Railroad

See Chapter on Railroads for the Middleburgh and Schoharie Railroad information. The Palatine house museum is open Saturdays and Sundays from noon in season {Memorial Day through Columbus Day}. Your visit includes a scarecrow, a nature walk, a cemetery walk, and the living history museum. Plan on one to three hours.

Palatine House 1743 Museum
102 Warner Hill Road,
Schoharie, NY 12157
42.661452, -74.308358

Peppermint Museum

Open Wednesday and Saturday afternoon this 1841 building houses the history and some of the machinery used for the making of peppermint oils.

> "H.G. Hotchkiss Essential Oil Co. Began on this site 1841. Awarded international medals making Lyons one of world's largest producers of Peppermint oil.. William C. Pomeroy Foundation 2015"

Plan on one hour.

95 Water Street,
Lyons, NY 14489
43.062871, -76.996214

Phelps Mansion Museum

Open Friday, Saturday, and Sunday this 1871 home is now open to the public as a museum that can be toured. *Judge Phelps* was a banker and established the *Susquehanna Valley Bank*, he died in 1878 and the building was passed on to family members. Plan on one hour.

191 Court Street
Binghamton, NY 13901
42.100665, -75.905566 M

Porter Hall - The Karpeles Manuscript Library Museum

Closed on Mondays. If you like old maps of the world, or beautiful stain-glass window, or a multi-pipe organ, then you may like visiting this 'Library Museum'.

Plan on 20 minutes to view the building's interior, more if looking at all the maps and other documents.

453 Porter Ave,
Buffalo, NY 14201
42.902383, -78.885876

Richardson Bates House Museum

Open Thursday, Friday, and Saturday afternoons as you enter this mansion you will gasp at the elegance of the furnishings, and marvel at the detailed woodwork that makes up the floors, walls, and ceilings. Plan on one-hour minimum.

135 E 3rd Street,

Oswego, NY 13126
43.455524, -76.503704

Richfield Springs Historic Association & Museum

Open noon to 4pm daily this museum provides a look at the *Cherry Valley Highway* and the *Mohawk Valley* of yesteryear. Plan on 30 minutes.

Richfield Springs Historic Association & Museum
134 W Main Street,
Richfield Springs, NY 13439
42.853346, -74.985942

Roberson Museum and Science Center

Roberson Museum and Science Center
Closed on Monday and Tuesday this center has a nice HO train layout, and planetarium along with various rooms that are specific to a subject like the *'Haudenosaunee* {People of the Longhouse} exhibit, and the *Earth From Space* area.

30 Front Street,
Binghamton, NY 13905
42.094015, -75.918656

Rochester Auto Museum

Call phone on their website for opening information. The museum has one or two vehicles that date back to the 1929 era, but most are Pontiac and Chrysler muscle cars from the 1960 to 1970 era. Plan on one or more hours.

Rochester Auto Museum
140 E Main Street,

Rochester, NY 14604
43.156876, -77.608422

Rochester Contemporary Art Center

Rochester Contemporary Art Center (RoCo)
Closed on Monday and Tuesday, open from noon on
other days this art center features hundreds of pieces of
picture art, some statues, and several 'out there' pieces
of contemporary artwork. Plan on two or more hours.

137 East Ave,
Rochester, NY 14604
43.156409, -77.600833

Rochester Medical Museum and Archives

Baker-Cederberg Museum

Closed on Saturday and Sunday this medical museum may be
more for the medical student or those that wish to study the
background of diseases and cures.

From the Official website.

"The Rochester Medical Museum and Archive is located at 1441 East Avenue at the Rochester Academy of Medicine Our collections include The Baker-Cederberg Museum and Archives of the Rochester General Hospital, The Genesee Hospital, Myers Community Hospital, Behavioral Health (Rochester Mental Health Center) Collection plus several tenant collections including: The New York State and Genesee Dietetic Associations and the Society for Total Emergency Programs (STEP) in one location. This consortium of Archives represent the vast array of Rochester's Healthcare -- some nineteen collections in all. You enter the museum from the second floor elevator to the gallery. This gallery was designed with temporary exhibits: photos, art and historical vignettes in mind."

Plan on one hour to all day or more.

Rochester Medical Museum and Archives
1441 East Ave,
Rochester, NY 14610
43.147482, -77.566007

Rochester Museum & Science Center

This museum is housed on three floors and has everything from dinosaur skeletons to a planetarium, including lots of activities for the younger visitors like a 'climbing wall', and other hands-on items.

Plan on three or more hours.

Rochester Engineering Society, Inc.

657 East Ave,
Rochester, NY 14607
43.152470, -77.587450

Russian History Museum

Holy Trinity Monastery

See the official website for opening times, the museum
was closed in June 2019 for upgrades, and opening is
expected to by in July.

The *Bolshevik* executed *Nicholas II* on July 17, 1918, Russia's last
tsar, and his family. This museum presents the history of the tsar
and his family and how his reign ended so brutally. The exhibits
include pictures, clothing, and the *Romanoff-owned Faberge works*

Plan on one to two hours.

Holy Trinity Monastery
1407 Robinson Road,
Mohawk, NY 13407
42.927196, -74.934418

Shacksboro Schoolhouse Museum

Opens at noon, closed on Monday and Tuesday. This
1879 school was used into the 1950 when state laws
required 'water' and it had none. It became a storage
building for a time, and eventually moved to the
current location and converted into a local history
museum. Plan on 15 minutes.

46 Canton Street,
Baldwinsville, NY 13027
43.151698, -76.334478

Salt Museum

Open on Saturday and Sunday the guides are in period garb and will provide you with the history of the 'Salt' mining and manufacturing industry of Onondaga Lake region of New York State. Plan on an hour.

106 Lake Drive,
Liverpool, NY 13088
43.099748, -76.206820

Schoharie Colonial Heritage

Schoharie Colonial Heritage Association
Contact them for opening times. This organization has the history of the 1743 Palatine House and the local railroads of the 1800s. Plan on one-half hour at the Palatine House, and another half-hour the restored 1891 passenger car.

See Chapter on Railroads and RR Museum for more info about the Middleburgh & Schoharie Railroad.

143 Depot Lane,
Schoharie, NY 12157
42.671564, -74.310595

Schoharie Easter Egg Museum

Badglet Museum Annex

Old Stone Fort Museum

Cobleskill Creek Covered Bridge

The *Badglet Museum Annex*, the *Old Stone Fort Museum*, the *Cobleskill Creek Covered Bridge*, and the *Easter Egg Museum* are all within feet of each other near *Lily Park*. Plan on one to two hours.

Schoharie Easter Egg Museum
112 Covered Bridge Road,
Schoharie, NY 12157
42.679624, -74.301808

Science Discovery Center

Closed Sunday, Monday, and Tuesday.

From the official website:

> "SUNY Oneonta's A.J. Read Science Discovery Center is a free, hands-on museum for people of all ages and abilities. Our mission is to connect visitors to the joy and power of the scientific process through authentic, interactive exhibits, and to serve as the indispensable Science, Technology, Engineering, Arts and Math (STEAM) resource for the SUNY Oneonta community and the wider region."

Plan on as many hours as you desire up to about 7-hours per day.

Science Discovery Center
Physical Science Building,
Oneonta, NY 13820
42.466884, -75.064808

Seneca Museum of Waterways and Industry

Closed on Sunday and Monday. This multistory museum is the town's visitor center on the street level, and the canal boat visitor center on the lower level. The museum tells about the various industrial plants that were once in Seneca Falls, and the way the canal helped establish the town and the industries. Plan on one hour or more. Note that there are several other museums and attractions in close proximity and therefore you should plan on a full day in Seneca Falls.

89 Fall Street,
Seneca Falls, NY 13148
42.910173, -76.797768

Seward House Museum

Seward's Folly

Closed on Sunday and Monday this Auburn museum was the home of politician *William Henry Seward* who had a very interesting career as New York State Senator, Governor of New York, a U.S. Senator, and as Secretary of State in the Lincoln and Johnson administrations. He is known for *Seward's Folly*, the purchase in 1867 of some *God Forsaken Land* in the far northwest, currently named *'Alaska'*. PS. In 1898 Gold was discovered and much later oil; things sometimes do work out for the good, Russia's loss. Plan on one hour at the mansion.

33 South Street,
Auburn, NY 13021
42.929648, -76.566702

Shako:wi Cultural Center

Oneida Indian Nation

Open Mondays, Wednesdays and Fridays from 9 a.m. to 5 p.m. Seasonal hours on Saturdays. Natives from several different tribes have settled this area of New York for over a thousand years. Over the centuries the tribes intermarried and became new tribes (new names) until we have the tribes of today. This cultural center tells much of the history of these proud peoples, and what is today considered the *Oneida Indian Nation*. Plan on one hour or more.

Shako:wi Cultural Center
5 Territory Road,
Oneida, NY 13421

43.039911, -75.621541

Spencerport Depot & Canal Museum

Rochester Lockport and Buffalo Interurban Trolley

Open 7 days a week from June to September and select hours in May and October. When one sees the word *'Depot'* one thinks of trains, i.e. a railroad depot and thus, may be confused by the name of this museum that is on the Erie Canal but nowhere near a train track. Well the building was actually part of the *Rochester Lockport and Buffalo interurban trolley line* from 1908 to 1931 and was donated to the town for *'useful purposes'*. I do believe it is doing its job. Plan on one hour and if traveling the canal by boat, bike, or foot, then stop in as they have bathroom facilities including showers.

Spencerport Depot & Canal Museum
16 East Ave,
Spencerport, NY 14559
43.192297, -77.799523

Stickley Museum

Onondaga Shops

L. & J.G Stickley Inc

Open Tuesday and Sunday this museum is a cabinet and furniture maker's exhibit. You can see and feel the mastery of how this factory turned lumber into fine artistic pieces of furniture, and as a bonus you can sit in a *"Dalai Lama Chair"*. Plan on one hour.

300 Orchard Street,
Fayetteville, NY 13066
43.025609, -76.006890

Susan B. Anthony Museum & House

19th Amendment

The Susan B. Anthony *'birthplace'* museum is in Massachusetts; closed on Mondays this is her home after she became an adult and participated in the *'Women's Suffrage Association'* that resulted in the *Women's Right to Vote in 1921*. In 1872 she did vote, and was promptly arrested for doing so; this led to her life changing and the results became history with the *19th Amendment* to the U.S. Constitution. Unfortunately, she never saw the results of her years of diligence as she passed away in 1906.

She is on US dollar coin that was minted from 1979 to 1981; then suspended, and returned to minting and circulation in 1999.

Plan on one hour or more.

Susan B. Anthony Museum & House
17 Madison Street,

Rochester, NY 14608
43.153190, -77.628064

Tennie Burton Museum

Open on Sundays during season. The museum provides some history of the town of Lima, New York dating back to the 1800s. Plan on 45 minutes.

Lima Historical Society
1850 Rochester Street,
Lima, NY 14485
42.906870, -77.612371

The Buffalo History Museum

Closed on Mondays this museum building looks to be straight out of Washington D.C. as its architecture resembles a courthouse, and there is a statue of *President Lincoln* at its entry. The museum is in a park like setting on *Holt Lake* near the *Japanese Gardens, Scajaquada Pathway,* and the location of the *Buffalo Cherry Blossom Festival.*

Inside you will see much, including a model train layout, military machine gun nest, a locomotive, Native American dioramas, lighthouse prism, coaches, and other artifacts of the history of Buffalo. Plan on two or more hours.

The Buffalo History Museum
1 Museum Court,
Buffalo, NY 14216
42.935419, -78.876269

The Cave House Museum of Mining & Geology

See the write-up on Howes Caverns; this is part of the complex.

The Cave House Museum of Mining & Geology
139 Blowing Rock Road,
Howes Cave, NY 12092
42.691363, -74.384428

The Farmers' Museum

Empire State Carousel

Bump Tavern

Todd's General Store

Open daily your visit will include *Todd's General Store, the Empire State Carousel,* and the *Bump Tavern* are some of the buildings at this 1840s living history museum and farm. There are cattle, sheep, goats, turkey, and other animals to see, as well as how life was lived in the 1800s in this region of New York State. Plan on three to four hours or more.

The Farmers' Museum
5775 NY-80,
Cooperstown, NY 13326
42.714943, -74.928366

The Lansing Manor House

Mine Kill State Park

Blenheim-Gilboa Project

Open daily this is near the *Schoharie Creek, Mine Kill State Park* and is part of the *New York State Blenheim-Gilboa Project Power Plant.* There is a visitor center and then the *Lansing Manor* house, which is the farmhouse that existed there before the power plant. Plan on one hour.

The Lansing Manor House
NY-30,
North Blenheim, NY 12131
42.448842, -74.464157

The Rockwell Museum

Open Daily this museum in Corning, New York is near the *Corning Glass Works Museum* and you should plan on seeing both during a full day's stay.

As you approach the building, look up, you will see the head of a buffalo sticking out of the side of the building; this is an indication of the exhibits of Native American, Wild Western, and the guns that won the west that you will see upon entry. Note, you may take photos, but may NOT use a flash. Plan on two to four hours.

111 Cedar Street,
Corning, NY 14830
42.142640, -77.052870

The Strong Museum

See the National Museum of Play

Open daily this is a museum of toys for girls and boys of all ages. Plan on one or more hours.

1 Manhattan Square Drive
Rochester, NY 14607
43.153034, -77.600876

Tinker Homestead & Farm Museum

Closed on Sunday and Monday. This farm has been turned into a nature park with trails. Plan on one or more hours.

Tinker Homestead & Farm Museum
1585 Calkins Road,
Pittsford, NY 14534
43.068622, -77.575411

Utica Children's Museum

Closed on Monday, Tuesday, and Wednesday this is a typical children's museum with tons of adventurous activities for the young. Plan on a few hours.

311 Main Street,
Utica, NY 13501
43.104301, -75.223996

Van Alstyne Homestead Museum

Open Saturdays from one to four. This is said to be the oldest building in the town of Canajoharie.

Marker inscription

"Built 1749 By Martin J. Van Alstyne. 16 of 31 Meetings of Tryon County Safety Committee Held Here 1774-75. General Nicholas Herkimer Received Commission As Brig. Gen Here 1775"

Plan on 45 minutes.

42 Moyer Street,
Canajoharie, NY 13317
42.903641, -74.572187

Walter Elwood Museum

Closed on Saturday and Sunday. This museum almost disappeared due to hurricane and flood damage, but is now reopened. From the official website.

"The exhibit includes five interactive stations where children and families can experience how Mr. Elwood studied. It allows for a changing selection of objects in our collection- from button collections, to hand-made doll clothes, to glass teaching slides to political buttons to fossils and shells.

Plan on one hour.
100 Church Street,
Amsterdam, NY 12010
42.939589, -74.184872

Wonderful Life Museum, Seneca

Bedford Falls

Closed on Sunday and Monday this is the real life *Bedford* Falls that was the basis for *It's a Wonderful Life*, the movie. The museum has tons of memorabilia on this movie and others. Plan on one or more hours.

32 Fall Street,
Seneca Falls, NY 13148
42.910433, -76.795391

Chapter # 12 – Niagara Falls

Niagara Falls consist of *Horseshoe Falls* on the Canadian side of the International border, and *American Falls* on the US side of the border. Most US citizens only go to the US side since they need a US Passport to go to the Canadian side and return. Here are some of the American side attractions that a visitor can partake on the US side.

Black Rock Lock - Niagara River

3 Dann Street,
Buffalo, NY 14207
42.935054, -78.907208

Buffalo Niagara Heritage Village

3755 Tonawanda Creek Road,
Amherst, NY 14228
43.084279, -78.729066

Cave of the Winds

Niagara Falls, NY 14303
43.082346, -79.070869

Wooden Walkway Near and Under the Falls (Shown)

Niagara Falls, NY 14303
43.083691, -79.071283

Duty Free Americas - Niagara Falls Rainbow Bridge Plaza

1 Rainbow Bridge Plaza,
Niagara Falls, NY 14303
43.089122, -79.064701

Gray Line Tours of Niagara Falls

1625 Buffalo Ave Suite 1A,
Niagara Falls, NY 14303

43.082360, -79.041108

Hells Half Acre

Niagara Falls
New York 14303
43.084284, -79.067014

Little Lady Liberty

413 Main Street,
Niagara Falls, NY 14301
43.088539, -79.063420

Maid of the Mist Boat Tour

1 Prospect Street,
Niagara Falls, NY 14303
43.086499, -79.067825

Niagara Civil War Monument

Unnamed Road,
Niagara Falls, NY 14303
43.085801, -79.065264

Niagara Falls Armory

901 Main Street,
Niagara Falls, NY 14301
43.097773, -79.053828

Niagara Falls Fireworks Displays

Prospect Street,

Niagara Falls, NY 14303
43.086443, -79.067234

Niagara Falls Observation Tower

332 Prospect Street,
Niagara Falls, NY 14303
43.086912, -79.068790

Niagara Falls USA Official Visitor Center & Destination Niagara USA Offices

10 Rainbow Blvd,
Niagara Falls, NY 14303
43.084488, -79.061994

Niagara Gorge Discovery Center

Niagara Falls, NY 14303
43.093513, -79.062164

Niagara Power Vista

5777 Lewiston Road,
Lewiston, NY 14092
43.140499, -79.038983

Niagara Wax Museum of History

303 Prospect Street,
Niagara Falls, NY 14303
43.086321, -79.064511

Nikola Tesla Monument

Goat Island Road,
Niagara Falls, NY 14303
43.082062, -79.071074

Old Stone Chimney

Niagara Falls, NY 14303
43.079032, -79.045348

Orin Lehman Visitor Center

Niagara Falls Visitor Center

Niagara Falls, NY 14303
43.086317, -79.066445

Parking Areas at the US side of Niagara Falls

There are several parking areas around the Niagara Falls tourist areas, and some have EV {Electric Vehicle} charging stations. Most are at ground level and out in the open. Caution, while it is nice to park under the trees in Lot # 3, the trees do during times of the year drop lots of sap {First hand-experience}. There is one multi-level public parking lot, and there are lots of parking if you are staying at one of the many motel or hotels in the area.

ChargePoint Charging Station - Lot # 1

350 Prospect Street,

Niagara Falls, NY 14303
43.086973, -79.065837

ChargePoint Charging Station - Lot # 2

Goat Island Road,
Niagara Falls, NY 14303
43.081546, -79.070424

Fishing Platform Parking Lot

Power Auth Service Road,
Niagara Falls, NY 14305
43.140004, -79.041380

Niagara Falls Parking Ramps – Multi-story Lot

40 Rainbow Blvd,
Niagara Falls, NY 14303
43.087752, -79.062998

Niagara Falls Visitor Center Parking Lot 1

Niagara Falls, NY 14303
43.087406, -79.064914

Niagara Falls Parking Lot 2

Goat Island Road,
Niagara Falls, NY 14303
43.081257, -79.070901

Niagara Falls Parking Lot 3

Niagara Falls, NY 14303
43.079410, -79.061397

Rainbow Air Inc

454 Main Street,
Niagara Falls, NY 14301
43.089630, -79.063051

Seneca Niagara Resort & Casino

700 Falls Street,
Niagara Falls, NY 14303
43.086466, -79.054191

Terrapin Point

Goat Island

Niagara Falls, NY 14303
43.080084, -79.074407

Three Sisters Islands

Niagara Falls, NY 14303
43.078092, -79.066057

U.S. Customs and Border Protection – Rainbow Bridge Port of Entry

302 Rainbow Blvd,
Niagara Falls, NY 14303
43.088240, -79.065644

Chapter # 13 – Niagara Falls – Canada

If you are going to Niagara Falls, then take your *Passport* and cross any of the bridges into Canada and spend a few hours to a day or two enjoying all the fun things on that side of the falls. Here is a short listing of some of the places to visit; most are self-explanatory.

{Picture is of Horseshoe Falls (Canadian Falls), it is from Wikipedia and is   public domain.}

Aquarium of Niagara

Niagara Falls, ON L2E 7M7, Canada
43.094315, -79.060138

Aquarium of Niagara Parking

Aquarium of Niagara, Niagara Falls, ON L2E 7M7, Canada
43.094315, -79.060139

Bird Kingdom - Canada

5651 River Road, Niagara Falls, ON L2E 7M7, Canada
43.092622, -79.068718

Burch's Mill Landmark

Former Toronto Power Generating Station

7230 Niagara Pkwy,
Allanburg,
ON L0S 1A0, Canada
43.071927, -79.073839

Casino Niagara - Canada

5705 Falls Ave,
Niagara Falls,
ON L2E 6T3, Canada
43.092122, -79.072673

Castle Dracula Wax Museum

4933 Clifton Hill,
Niagara Falls,
ON L2G 3N5, Canada
43.091363, -79.074339

Circus World Display Inc

5681 Victoria Ave,
Niagara Falls,
ON L2G 3L5, Canada
43.092739, -79.075341

Dinosaur Adventure Golf

4952 Clifton Hill,
Niagara Falls,

ON L2G 3N4, Canada
43.090481, -79.075885

Fallsview Casino

5705 Falls Ave,
Niagara Falls,
ON L2E 6T3, Canada
43.082047, -79.080815

Great Canadian Midway

4850 Clifton Hill,
Niagara Falls,
ON L2G 3N4, Canada
43.090957, -79.074450

Journey Behind the Falls

This is a tour {walk} behind *Horseshoe Falls* in a series of caves that allow you to look out through the waterfall from behind it.

6650 Niagara Pkwy,
Niagara Falls,
ON L2E 3E8, Canada
43.079336, -79.078589

Louis Tussaud's Waxworks

5709 Victoria Ave,
Niagara Falls,
ON L2G 3L5, Canada
43.092564, -79.076119

Movieland Wax Museum Niagara Falls

4950 Clifton Hill,
Niagara Falls,
ON L2G 3N4, Canada
43.090923, -79.074019

Old Scow Lookout Point

7530 Niagara Pkwy,
Niagara Falls,
ON L0S 1A0, Canada
43.070686, -79.071952

Rock Legends Wax Museum

5020 Centre Street,
Niagara Falls,
ON L2G 3N7, Canada
43.092163, -79.076652

The Haunted House

Clifton Hill,
Niagara Falls,
ON L2G 3N5, Canada
43.091242, -79.074155

Upside Down House

4967 Clifton Hill,
Niagara Falls,
ON L2G 3N5, Canada
43.092268, -79.074922

Whirlpool Aero Car

3850 Niagara Pkwy
Niagara Falls,
ON L2E 3E8, Canada
43.118030, -79.068800

WildPlay Niagara Falls MistRider Zipline

5920 Niagara Pkwy,
Niagara Falls,
ON L2E 6X8, Canada
43.088885, -79.073623

Chapter # 14 – State & Federal Parks

The only Federal Parks in the area is the *Women's*

Rights National Historical Park in Seneca Falls, New York and the *Saratoga National Historical Park* in Saratoga, New York; the other parks in the area are Local Township, County, or State Parks. Here is a short listing and it is not all-inclusive.

{NPS Picture from Wikipedia of the Wesleyan Chapel in the Women's Rights National Historical park, it is public domain}

Many of the parks have local maps, hiking trails; wooded areas, pond, and some have lakes with public beaches.

Note that some of the state parks have facilities for camping and for RV camping, but many are only open during the daylight hours so check with each park before making the visit.

1 Hamlin Beach State Park

Hamlin, NY 14464
43.360069, -77.954034

Cayuga Lake State Park

2678 Lower Lake Road,
Seneca Falls, NY 13148
42.896132, -76.754039

Cayuga Lake State Park-East

Willows Hill Road,
Seneca Falls, NY 13148
42.896042, -76.752132

Chenango Valley State Park

Park Office
Chenango Forks, NY 13746
42.213568, -75.830035

De Veaux Woods State Park

3180 De Veaux Woods Drive E,

Niagara Falls, NY 14305
43.119246, -79.061102

Delta Lake State Park

8797 NY-46,
Rome, NY 13440
43.290617, -75.416331

Finger Lakes Region State Park
Headquarters

2221 Taughannock Park Road,
Trumansburg, NY 14886
42.542639, -76.606166

Fort Niagara State Park

1 Scott Ave,
Youngstown, NY 14174
43.260880, -79.054750

Old Fort Niagara

102 Morrow Plaza,
Youngstown, NY 14174
43.262372, -79.060627

Old Fort Niagara Light, Youngstown, NY

Fort Niagara State Park,
Scott Ave,
Youngstown, NY 14174
43.261767, -79.060519

Four Mile Creek State Park

1055 Lake Road,
Youngstown, NY 14174
43.274220, -78.997468

Glimmerglass State Park

Glimmerglass State Park
1527 County Road 31,
Cooperstown, NY 13326
42.786610, -74.862220

Hyde Hall Covered Bridge

Glimmerglass State Park,
Cooperstown, NY 13326
42.790169, -74.863425

Hyde Hall Museum

267 Glimmerglass State Park,
Cooperstown, NY 13326
42.793416, -74.873235

Sleeping Lion Hiking Trail

Cooperstown, NY 13326
42.793226, -74.876899

Joseph Davis State Park

Youngstown, NY 14174
43.213896, -79.039069

Fishing Dock - Joseph Davis State Park

4094 Lower River Road,
Youngstown, NY 14174
43.215005, -79.051247

Lakeside Beach State Park

13691 Roosevelt Hwy,
Waterport, NY 14571
43.366839, -78.235878

Long Point State Park

4459 NY-430
Bemus Point, NY 14712
42.180191, -79.412849

Newtown Battlefield State Park

2346 County Rd 60,
Elmira, NY 14901
42.046136, -76.733946

Saratoga National Historical Park - NPS

648 NY-32,
Stillwater, NY 12170
43.012283, -73.648947

Thompson's Lake State Park

East Berne, NY 12059
42.652755, -74.049109

Upper Buttermilk Falls State Park

Unnamed Road,
Ithaca, NY 14850
42.409317, -76.512318

Watkins Glen State Park Six Nations Camping Area

This State Park has six camping areas that represent the Native American tribes of the area's present and past as follows:

Cayuga Village, Oneida Village, Mohawk Village, Onondaga Village, Seneca Village, & Tuscarora Village

1009 N Franklin Street,
Watkins Glen, NY 14891
42.370520, -76.882378

Watkins Glen State Park, Upper Entrance

3310 NY-409,
Watkins Glen, NY 14891
42.373570, -76.891934

Chapter # 15 – RV Parks

There may be dozens of parks in this area of New York  State that have the facilities for Recreational Vehicles (RVs), but they are not named as such. This listing is, and therefore each of the following camping areas should have the proper electrical, water, and plumbing hookup that is required of an RV camper. Check with state and federal parks as many do have proper facilities. The chapter on campgrounds list many campgrounds that may have RV support, but usually camping in those camps is limited to tent camping and thus may NOT have the proper hookups. You need to contact the camps to see if they have the facilities you desire.

Brennan Beach RV Resort

80 Brennan Beach Road,
Pulaski, NY 13142
43.579713, -76.181101

Brookview RV Park & Camping

8108 Green Road,
Hubbardsville, NY 13355
42.817037, -75.461700

Butternut Hill RV Camping

6893 Hwy 20,
Bouckville, NY 13310
42.891671, -75.542230

Cross Lake Campground & RV Park

12946 Duger Road,
Cato, NY 13033
43.154100, -76.484907

Fire Fox Resorts Golf Course & RV Park

330 Rabbit Path Road,
Lisle, NY 13797
42.279795, -76.024777

Hejamada Campground & RV Park

748 McDonald Road,
Port Byron, NY 13140
42.996225, -76.688873

Hillcrest RV Sales & Service

72 E Service Road
Binghamton, NY 13901
42.147011, -75.891187

Holiday Harbor RV Park

9415 Blind Sodus Bay Road,
Red Creek, NY 13143
43.336127, -76.736825

Jellystone Park of Western New York

5204 Youngers Road,
North Java, NY 14113
42.642241, -78.315986

Jones Pond Men's Only Campground & RV Park

9835 Old State Road,
Angelica, NY 14709
42.427501, -77.970363

Maple Lane RV Park

9272, 5233 Maple Lane,
Cuba, NY 14727
42.227314, -78.277870

MorningStar RV Park

11924 Townley Hill Road,
Corning, NY 14830
42.214477, -76.974605

Oneida Indian Nation RV Park

5065 NY-365,
Verona, NY 13478
43.105489, -75.604590

Pine Valley RV Park & Campground

600 Boswell Hill Road,

Endicott, NY 13760
42.145711, -76.089618

Port Bay RV Park & Campgrounds

8346 E Port Bay Road,
Wolcott, NY 14590
43.299713, -76.827275

Red Rock Ponds RV Resort

16097 Canal Road,
Holley, NY 14470
43.255173, -78.077067

RV Park New York

56 Creamery Road,
Callicoon, NY 12723
41.761639, -75.054441

South Shore RV Park

7867 Lake Road
Sodus Point, NY 14555
43.269637, -77.010268

Streamside RV Park and Golf Course

800 County Rte 28,
Pulaski, NY 13142
43.508039, -76.111023

Sunset RV Park Inc

6018 61, Co Rte 89,
Oswego, NY 13126
43.449520, -76.556204

Treasure Isle RV Park

3132 Haskins Road,
Blossvale, NY 13308
43.231355, -75.676573

Twilight on the Erie RV Resort

1100 Marina Pkwy,
Macedon, NY 14502
43.077130, -77.328037

Villages RV Park At Turning Stone

5065 NY-365,
Verona, NY 13478
43.106708, -75.606603

Wildwood Lakes Campground and RV Park

14607 Cayuga Street,
Sterling, NY 13156
43.323694, -76.699064

Chapter # 16 – Tours and Commercial Trips

This chapter has some of the many commercial tours that you may seek; it is NOT all-inclusive and no company has paid or otherwise sought out a listing in this travel book. You as the reader have to decide which companies you desire to contract; and you may find others that are unlisted that are more to your liking.

{Picture from Wikipedia, author Mccallusa. This is a tour boat on the Erie canal, it is public domain}

1st Choice Fishing Charters

175 N Water Street,
Lewiston, NY 14092
43.174474, -79.049104

Bohringer's Fruit Farm

~The Fydenkevez Family~ Joe, Susan, and Emily
3992 NY-30,
Middleburgh, NY 12122
42.588436, -74.359618

Buffalo Charter/Miss Buffalo

Ferry type boat ride down the Buffalo River and the Buffalo Harbor. Plan on two hours.

79 Marine Drive
Buffalo, NY 14202
42.878625, -78.885436

Cave of the Winds

Niagara Falls, NY 14303
43.082346, -79.070869

Center at High Falls

Brown's-Race Historic District

Closed on Saturday and Sundays this walking tour of High Falls Brown's-Race Historic District.. The location provides a good look at the 96-foot high waterfall on the Genesee River.

Center At High Falls
60 Browns Race # 1,
Rochester, NY 14614
43.161288, -77.616494

Drab6 Fishing Charters

104 N Water Street,
Lewiston, NY 14092
43.173234, -79.048857

Dutch Apple Cruises & Tours

1002 141 Broadway,
Albany, NY 12202
42.641977, -73.750522

Erie Canal Cruises

New York
43.017019, -74.997471

Glenville Oktoberfest - Main Biergarten

Maalwyck Park Road,
Schenectady, NY 12302
42.830963, -73.988550

Gold Standard Equestrian Center

7261 Vienna Road,
Blossvale, NY 13308
43.213815, -75.719460

Gray Line Tours of Niagara Falls

1625 Buffalo Ave Suite 1A,
Niagara Falls, NY 14303
43.082360, -79.041108

Hunter Landing Equestrian

3207 Haskins Road,
Blossvale, NY 13308
43.237264, -75.677280

Journey Behind the Falls

6650 Niagara Pkwy,
Niagara Falls,
ON L2E 3E8, Canada
43.079336, -79.078589

Madison County Hop Fest

435 Main Street,
Oneida, NY 13421
43.087620, -75.647300

Maid of the Mist Boat Tour

1 Prospect Street,
Niagara Falls, NY 14303
43.086499, -79.067825

Niagara Celtic Heritage Festival

6108 E Lake Road,
Burt, NY 14028
Lake Ontario
43.339868, -78.707557

NT Kayak Launch Facilities Botanical Gardens

1825 Sweeney Street,
North Tonawanda, NY 14120
43.037917, -78.827074

Rainbow Air Inc.

Helicopter rides above the falls. This experience is a once in a lifetime treat, and some have even gotten married in the Helicopter as it circled the falls. Plan on an hour or more for the tour, which spends from 10 to 20 minutes over the falls. There are extended tours, and you should make reservations in advance.

Note that there are other tour operators in the area.

454 Main Street,
Niagara Falls, NY 14301
43.089636, -79.063032

The Glimmerglass Festival

7300 NY-80,
Cooperstown, NY 13326
42.810568, -74.900515

Whirlpool Aero Car

3850 Niagara Pkwy
Niagara Falls,
ON L2E 3E8, Canada
43.118030, -79.068800

Whirlpool Jet Boat Tours

115 S Water Street,
Lewiston, NY 14092
43.172617, -79.049099

WildPlay Niagara Falls MistRider Zipline

5920 Niagara Pkwy,
Niagara Falls,
ON L2E 6X8, Canada
43.088885, -79.073623

Chapter # 17 – Train Rides and Railroad Museums

 The era of railroads took over the transportation of goods that were the lifeblood of the Erie and Barge canals, and the highways and airlines took over the lifeblood of the railroads.

{1902 Picture is from Wikipedia, it is public domain}

Today many of the railroads that crisscrossed the area are no longer in operation, but their footprints still remain in the form of abandoned depots, rail bridges, locomotives, rolling stock, and rail trails. Many of the depots have been converted to museums, the locomotives and rolling stock put on display, and the tracks removed to leave what are now *rail trails* for hiking and such.

There are also collectors and model builders that have salvaged items from the extinct railroads, or have built replicas of the towns and tracks in miniature scale. Many of these railroad items are listed here, and if you know of something I missed, leave a note on the Amazon book comments.

Arcade & Attica Railroad Corporation

This touring railroad offers a variety of rail trips from 35 miles to 80 miles or more and to different towns in the Buffalo, New York area. See their website for trip information and specials.

278 Main Street,
Arcade, NY 14009
42.533853, -78.423908

Buffalo Cattaraugus & Jamestown Scenic Railway

4 Scott Street,
Hamburg, NY 14075
42.719073, -78.842781

Cooperstown & Charlotte Valley Railroad

136 E Main Street
Milford, NY 13807
42.589518, -74.942124

D & H Building

353 Broadway,
Albany, NY 12246

42.648166, -73.750106

Delaware, Lackawanna & Western Railroad Station (Painted Post, New York)

Painted Post,
NY 14870
42.162321, -77.091023

Delaware & Ulster Railroad

Rides through the Catskill Mountains from Arkville to Roxbury and back on Saturdays and Sundays; pulled by restored steam or other engines

43510 NY-28,
Arkville, NY 12406
42.147580, -74.615884

Edgerton Model Railroad Club

"Model Railroad Heaven!"

Closed on Saturday and Sunday this 1950 model Railroad club was established by Governor Thomas E. Dewey.

Edgerton Recreation Center
41 Backus Street,
Rochester, NY 14608
43.171584, -77.632846

Empire State Railway Museum

70 Lower, High Street,
Phoenicia, NY 12464
42.080437, -74.308290

Rail Explorers: Catskills Division

70 High Street,
Phoenicia, NY 12464
42.080387, -74.308250

Former FJ&G Electric Railroad Carbarn

10 River Street,
Gloversville, NY 12078
43.042843, -74.350685

Fulton County Museum

Fonda, Johnstown and Gloversville Railroad

This is NOT the museum in Rochester, Indiana. This
museum is in Gloversville, New York and has the
FJ&G RR exhibit as well as information on the *leather
and glove business*es of the era and the way in which
the railroad aided it in the 1870s to the 1980s period.
Large model railroad layout is on display and is said to
be historically accurate. Plan on one to two hours.

239 Kingsboro Ave
Gloversville, NY 12078
43.065980, -74.336337

Leatherstocking Railway

136 E Main Street,
Milford, NY 13807
42.590007, -74.942131

Medina Railroad Museum

530 West Ave,
Medina, NY 14103
43.218379, -78.389739

Middleburgh and Schoharie Railroad

Schoharie Valley Railroad Museum

The *Schoharie Valley Railroad Museum* is open weekends 12PM to 4PM Memorial Day thru Columbus Day.

These are some of the last remaining rolling stock of the railroad and are open for your viewing. There is a restored 1891 passenger car and a 1917 wooden caboose along with some models and a 1920 scale model of buildings, cars and terrain of the railroad route.

The history of this railroad also includes the *1828 Albany & Susquehanna Railroad* that later became the *Delaware and Hudson Railroad*; and the *1867 Schoharie Valley Railroad*.

Plan on one hour.

Palatine House 1743 Museum
102 Warner Hill Road,

Schoharie, NY 12157
42.661452, -74.308358

Model Railroad Exhibits in other museums

See the following:
miSci - Museum of Innovation and Science
Roberson Museum and Science Center
The Buffalo History Museum

New York Museum of Transportation

6393 E River Road
West Henrietta, NY 14586
43.016728, -77.709795

Old Rolling Stock and Locomotives in other museums

See the following:
Schoharie Colonial Heritage
The Buffalo History Museum

Old Train Depots used for other museums.

See the following:

Long Homestead Historical Museum
Spencerport Depot & Canal Museum

Owego Harford Railway

Meridian Southern Railway
25 Delphine Street,
Owego, NY 13827

42.108144, -76.268927

Roberson Museum and Science Center

Roberson Museum and Science Center
Closed on Monday and Tuesday this center has a nice
HO train layout as well as many other subjects.

30 Front Street,
Binghamton, NY 13905
42.094015, -75.918656

Rochester & Genesee Valley Railroad Museum

282 Rush Scottsville Road,
Rush, NY 14543
43.003395, -77.721020

Schoharie Valley Railroad Museum

Schoharie Valley Railroad Museum
143 Depot Lane,
Schoharie, NY 12157
42.670242, -74.311127

Syracuse Amtrak Station

131 Alliance Bank Pkwy,
Syracuse, NY 13208
43.076556, -76.169244

Vestal Museum

Open Thursday, Friday, and Saturday this is an old *Railroad Depot* building that was moved to the town's library parking lot. The museum has items from the old station and has some of the history of the town. Plan on 30 minutes.

Vestal Museum
328 Vestal Pkwy E,
Vestal, NY 13850
42.087898, -76.045405

Chapter # 18 – Vineyards & Wineries at the Finger Lakes

The wine grapes of the Finger Lakes region are some of the finest in the world, and as it turned out, the rootstock was impervious to the *North American grape phylloxera* (aphids) that somehow were transported to France in the 1850s and nearly destroyed their entire wine industry. The Finger Lake rootstock was then used as the roots for the French grapes in France, thus allowing their wine industry to be reestablished.

{Picture from Wikipedia, author Pubdog, it is of the Gold Seal Winery. It is public domain}

The following listing of vineyards and wineries contain mostly wines from the Finger Lakes, but also many from other counties in upstate New York. Plan on an hour or two when visiting a vineyard, and be sure to check in advance to see when, or if, the winery you plan to visit will be open.

See the author's book on the Hudson Valley for its many fine wines and vineyards.

Americana Vineyards Winery

Americana Vineyards Winery
4367 E Covert Road,
Interlaken, NY 14847
42.575942, -76.677010

Atwater Estate Vineyards, LLC

Atwater Estate Vineyards, LLC
5055 NY-414,
Burdett, NY 14818
42.478502, -76.869325

Bloomer Creek Vineyard

Bloomer Creek Vineyard
5301 NY-414,
Hector, NY 14841
42.489695, -76.870008

Cayuga Ridge Estate Winery

6800 NY-89,
Ovid, NY 14521
42.694633, -76.743924

Deer Run Winery

3772 W Lake Road,
Geneseo, NY 14454
42.822710, -77.718846

Double A Vineyards, Inc.

10277 Christy Road,
Fredonia, NY 14063
42.448052, -79.296226

Dr. Konstantin Frank Winery

Dr. Konstantin Frank Winery
9749 Middle Road,
Hammondsport, NY 14840
42.473519, -77.184040

Fox Run Vineyards

Fox Run Vineyards
670 NY-14,
Penn Yan, NY 14527
42.731018, -76.972447

Gold Seal Winery

Permanently Closed

13404 W Lake Road
Hammondsport, NY 14840
42.502475, -77.157864

Hazlitt 1852 Vineyards

Hazlitt 1852 Vineyards
5712 NY-414,
Hector, NY 14841
42.510598, -76.876040

Hermann J. Wiemer Vineyard

Hermann J. Wiemer Vineyard
3962 NY-14,
Dundee, NY 14837
42.572025, -76.928100

Heron Hill Winery

Blue Heron Cafe
9301 Co Road 76,
Hammondsport, NY 14840
42.449629, -77.201394

Heron Hill Tasting Room on Seneca Lake

3586 NY-14,
Himrod, NY 14842
42.590602, -76.941370

Heron Hill Tasting Room at Canandaigua Lake

5323 Seneca Point Road,
Canandaigua, NY 14424
42.762122, -77.335350

Johnson Estate Winery

8419 E Main Street,
Westfield, NY 14787
42.307150, -79.606375

Keuka Lake Vineyards

Keuka Lake Vineyards
8882 County Road 76,
Hammondsport, NY 14840
42.431390, -77.199722

Keuka Spring Vineyards

Keuka Spring Vineyards
243 Route 54,
East Lake Road,
Penn Yan, NY 14527
42.626397, -77.067419

Knapp Winery & The Vineyard Restaurant

(Restaurant open April through November- Please call
for hours)
Knapp Winery & The Vineyard Restaurant, Note-
(Restaurant open April through November- Please call
for hours)

2770 Ernsberger Road,
Romulus, NY 14541
42.765169, -76.782689

Lake Erie Grape Discovery Center

8305 W, Hwy 20,
Westfield, NY 14787
42.310286, -79.597770

Lakewood Vineyards Inc

Lakewood Vineyards Inc
4024 NY-14,
Watkins Glen, NY 14891
42.428968, -76.906090

Lamoreaux Landing Wine Cellars

Lamoreaux Landing Wine Cellars
9224 NY-414,
Lodi, NY 14860
42.576640, -76.858455

Lucas Vineyards

Lucas Vineyards
8277 Dickerson Drive
Interlaken, NY 14847
42.627872, -76.710154

Montezuma Winery & Hidden Marsh Distillery

2981 Hwy 20,
Seneca Falls, NY 13148
42.950643, -76.767881

Ravines Wine Cellars

Ravines Wine Cellars
400 Barracks Road,
Geneva, NY 14456
42.844730, -77.000998

Sheldrake Point Winery

Sheldrake Point Winery
7448 County Road 153,
Ovid, NY 14521
42.663441, -76.701436

The Thirsty Owl Wine Company

6861 NY-89,
Ovid, NY 14521
42.693281, -76.741334

The Village Vineyard

467 Center Street,
Lewiston, NY 14092
43.189508, -79.040416

Ventosa Vineyards

Ventosa Vineyards
3440 NY-96A,
Geneva, NY 14456
42.857170, -76.936127

Wagner Vineyards Estate Winery

Wagner Vineyards Estate Winery
9322 NY-414,
Lodi, NY 14860
42.571859, -76.859364

Zugibe Vineyards

Zugibe Vineyards
4248 E Lake Road,
Geneva, NY 14456
42.819188, -76.931197

Chapter # 19 – Waterfalls

 New York State has lots of rain and snow, and therefore lots of streams (Creeks), and rivers. Therefore it is understandable that there would be plenty of waterfalls of all sizes and shapes, and this chapter presents the reader with several of the more interesting falls that have become 'tourist' attractions. *{Taughannock Falls shown}*

Aunt Sarahs Falls

Aunt Sarahs Falls
Montour Falls, NY 14891
42.350928, -76.858569

Brickyard Falls

Brickyard Falls
Pompey, NY 13104
42.985351, -75.986304

Bucktail Falls

Bucktail Falls
Spafford, NY 13141
42.822303, -76.241315

Buttermilk Falls

Buttermilk Falls State Park
112 E Buttermilk Falls Road,
Ithaca, NY 14850
42.417107, -76.521172

Carpenter Falls

Carpenter Falls
Niles, NY 13118
42.811743, -76.343269

Cascadilla Gorge Waterfall

Walkway to the gorge & its waterfall

Cascadilla Gorge Trail
Ithaca, NY 14850
42.442907, -76.494038

Clifton Falls

Clifton Falls
Ledyard, NY 13026
42.740092, -76.688830

Delphi Falls

Delphi Waterfall
Cazenovia, NY 13035
42.863994, -75.899220

Edwards Falls

Edwards Falls Park
4496 Limestone Drive,
Manlius, NY 13104
42.990265, -75.962203

Fellows Falls

Fellows Falls
Tully, NY 13159
42.816187, -76.157424

Forest Falls

Ithaca
New York 14850
42.452103, -76.488216

Glenora Falls

Glenora Falls
Starkey, NY 14837
42.490072, -76.916916

Hector Falls

Hector Falls
Hector, NY 14818
42.417863, -76.865238

Holley Canal Falls

Holley, NY 14470
43.225846, -78.019105

Honeoye Falls

New York
42.952032, -77.591503

Horseshoe Falls - Canada

North America - Canada
43.077329, -79.075356

Horseshoe Falls - Ithaca

Ithaca
New York 14850
42.452000, -76.485985

Hosmer Falls

Hosmer Falls
Romulus, NY 14521
42.685353, -76.739674

Ithaca Falls

Ithaca Falls
New York 14850
42.452806, -76.491712

Kings Falls

Kings Falls
Denmark, NY 13626
43.917017, -75.632967

Lower Falls – Enfield Glen

Ithaca
New York
42.397407, -76.561183

Lucifer Falls

Lucifer Falls
Enfield, NY 14850
42.400638, -76.584113

Montville Falls

Montville Falls
Moravia, NY 13118
42.717295, -76.409103

Moonshine Falls

Moonshine Falls
Ledyard, NY 13026
42.727032, -76.688281

Niagara Falls / American Falls

North America
43.084383, -79.069503

Oak Tree Falls

Oak Tree Falls
Ovid, NY 14521
42.676747, -76.729397

Old Mill Falls

Old Mill Falls
Upper Park Road,
Ithaca, NY 14850
42.401913, -76.589534

Parson Falls

Parson Falls
Moravia, NY 13118
42.722865, -76.451604

Pratts Falls

Pratts Falls
Pompey, NY 13104
42.931178, -75.994125

Rainbow Falls

Glen Creek
New York 14891
42.374293, -76.875886

Rexford Falls

Rexford Falls
Sherburne, NY 13460
42.678964, -75.471288

Rocky Falls

Ithaca
New York 14850

42.452076, -76.484480

Salmon River Falls

Salmon River Falls Unique Area
Falls Road,
Richland, NY 13144
43.547648, -75.940207

Secret Caverns

Underground waterfall

671 Caverns Road,
Howes Cave, NY 12092
42.709602, -74.391949

Shequaga Falls

Shequaga Falls Park
109 S Genesee Street,
Montour Falls, NY 14865
42.344900, -76.850177

Silver Thread Falls

Silver Thread Falls
Lodi, NY 14860
42.612855, -76.856072

Taughannock Falls

Taughannock Falls
Ulysses, NY 14886
42.535632, -76.610776

Taughannock Falls Overlook View Point

2381 Taughannock Park Road,
Trumansburg, NY 14886
42.538350, -76.607983

Tinker Falls

Tinker Falls
Tinker Falls Trail,
Tully, NY 13159
42.782565, -76.033127

Tinker's Falls Accessible Trail Parking

Tinker Falls Trail,
Tully, NY 13159
42.780238, -76.036195

Triphammer Falls

Ithaca
New York 14850
42.451571, -76.480353

VanBuskirk Falls

VanBuskirk Falls
VanBuskirk Road,
Newfield, NY 14867
42.331617, -76.552910

Appendix I – Towns covered in this Manual

New York Towns in this guidebook.

Albany	Altmar	Amherst
Angelica	Arkville	Auburn (Cayuga)
Avon	Barker	Batavia
Bethel Woods	Bridgeport	Binghamton (Broome County)
Blossvale	Bouckville	Buffalo
Burdett	Caledonia	Callicoon
Canajoharie (Montgomery)	Canandaigua	Canastota
Cape Vincent	Caroga Lake	Castile
Cazenovia	Charlotteville	Chenango Forks
Chittenango	Clifton Park	Cohoes
Cooperstown (Otsego County)	Corning	Cortland
Cuba	Dansville	Denmark
Dundee	Durhamville	East Berne
East Bloomfield	East Otto	East Syracuse (Onondaga)
Endicott (Broome County)	Fairport	Farmington
Fayetteville (Onondaga)	Fairport	Fly Creek
Fort Hunter (Montgomery)	Fort Plain (Montgomery)	Frankfort

Geneseo	Gilboa	Glenville
Gloversville	Hamburg	Hamlin
Hammondsport	Hector	Henrietta
Herkimer	Hilton	Himrod
Homer	Howes Cave	Hubbardsville
Ilion	Interlaken	Johnson City (Broome County)
Kent	Kirkville (Onondaga)	Lafayette
Ledyard	Lewiston	Lima
Little Falls	Liverpool (Onondaga)	Lockport
Lodi	Lowman	Macedon
Manlius (Onondaga)	Medina	Middleburgh (Schoharie County)
Middleville	Mohawk	Montour Falls
Moravia (Cayuga)	New Hartford	Newark
Newfield	Niagara Falls {Canada}	Nichols
Niles	Niskayuna	North Tonawanda
Olcott	Oneida	Oswego
Ovid	Painted Post	Palmyra
Penn Yan	Perry	Pittsford
Pompey	Red Creek	Rexford
Richland	Rochester	Rome
Romulus	Rush	Rotterdam Junction
Saratoga Springs	Seneca Falls	Schenectady
Schoharie	Scotia	Sherburne (Chenango County)

Sodus Point	Spafford	Spencer
Starkey	St Johnsville	Sterling
Stillwater	Sylvan Beach	Syracuse (Onondaga)
Trumansburg	Tully	Ulysses
Utica	Vernon	Verona
Victor	Waterford	Waterloo
Waterville	Watkins Glen	Westernville
Westfield	West Henrietta	Wolcott
Youngstown		

Appendix II – Native American Tribes

New York State has a long history of being settled by Native American {Indian} Tribes and as you travel the state you will encounter hundreds of towns, locations, rivers, lakes, etc., that carry the names, both current and ancient. Here are some of the tribes and reservations that are current or that existed when the 'White' men explored this area of the state. There are other tribes in the areas not covered by this book.

Tribes in 1600

Algonquian, Cayuga, Erie, Oneida, Onondaga, & Seneca

1600 to 1720

Cayuga - People of the Great Swamp
Mohawk - People of the Great Flint
Oneida - People of Standing Stone
Onondaga - People of the Hills

Seneca - People of the Great Hill
Tuscarora - Hemp Gatherers

1910 Indian Reservations

Allegany, Cattaraugus, Old Spring, Onondaga, St
Regis, Tonawanda, & Tuscarora

Current 2019

Oneida, Onondaga, Seneca, Shinnecock, St. Regis,
Tonawanda, Tuscarora, & Unkechaug

Index

Author

The author has lived in New York State for many years and has traveled the Niagara Falls to Albany area extensively. He has visited many of the attractions and museums that are in this touring guidebook. The author is also a researcher and has done extensive research on the area and its attributes; which is included in this text.

See all of the author's travel guides at the following links.

BorderTransportationSystem Travel Books

William (Bill) C. McElroy

Cover Picture

 This is a wooden walkway under the American Falls at Niagara Falls. You are issued rain gear, and then you take an elevator down to the bottom of the gorge and out onto the walkway. Trust me, you will get wet, but you will also admire the sound, strength, and tremendous view you can only get from the bottom of the falls.

CCF06172019_00001.jpg

Printed in Great Britain
by Amazon

17687902R00135